# ENCHANTED MENAGERIE

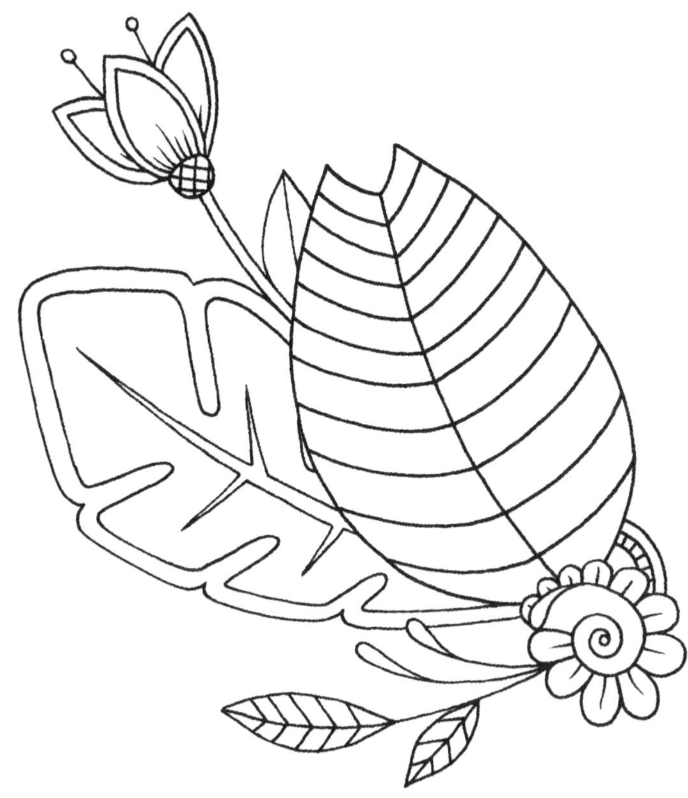

Maud Feral Chauveau

# Maud FERAL CHAUVEAU - (MFC)

## Enchanted Menagerie

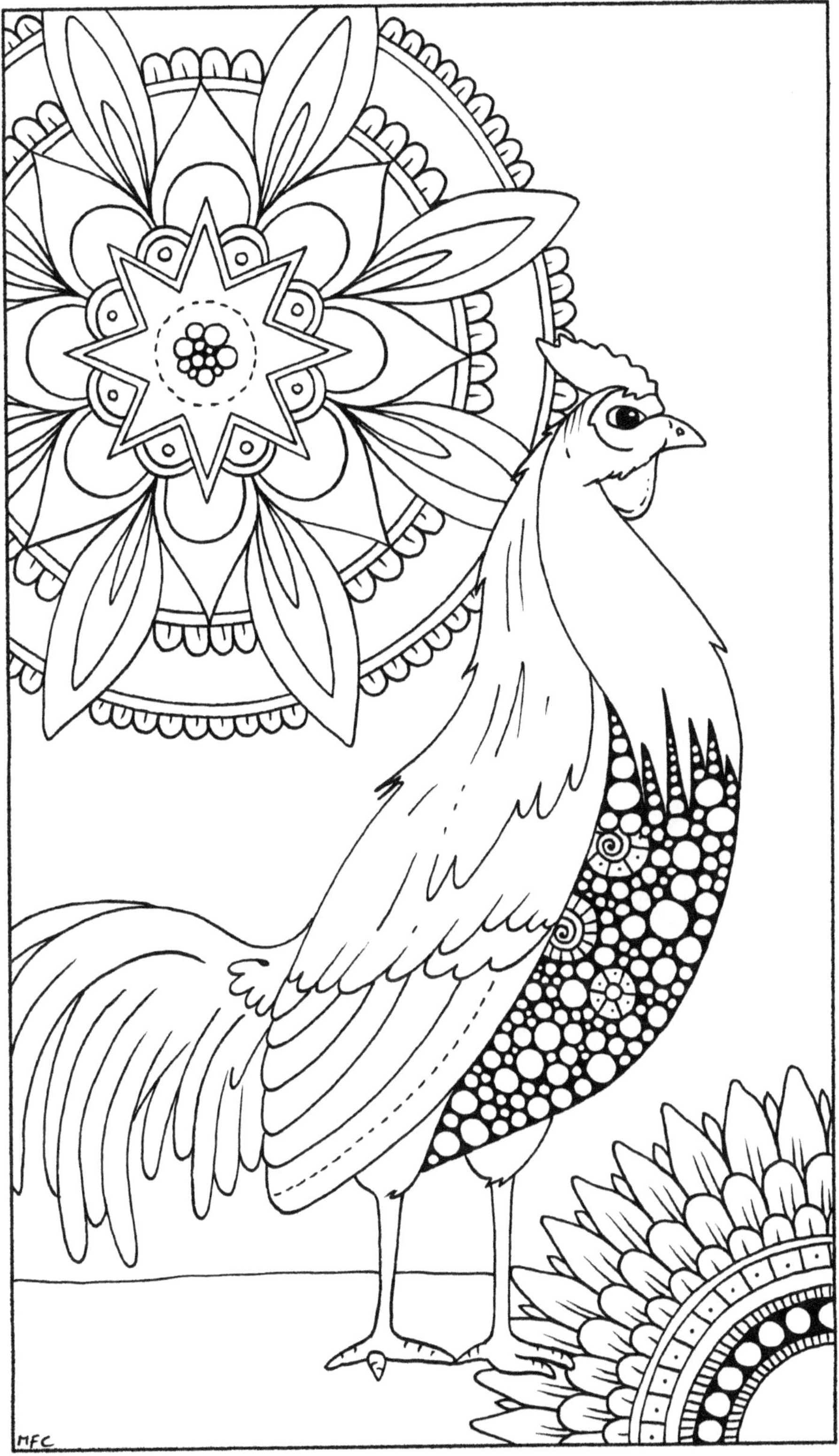

Maud FERAL CHAUVEAU - (MFC)

Enchanted Menagerie

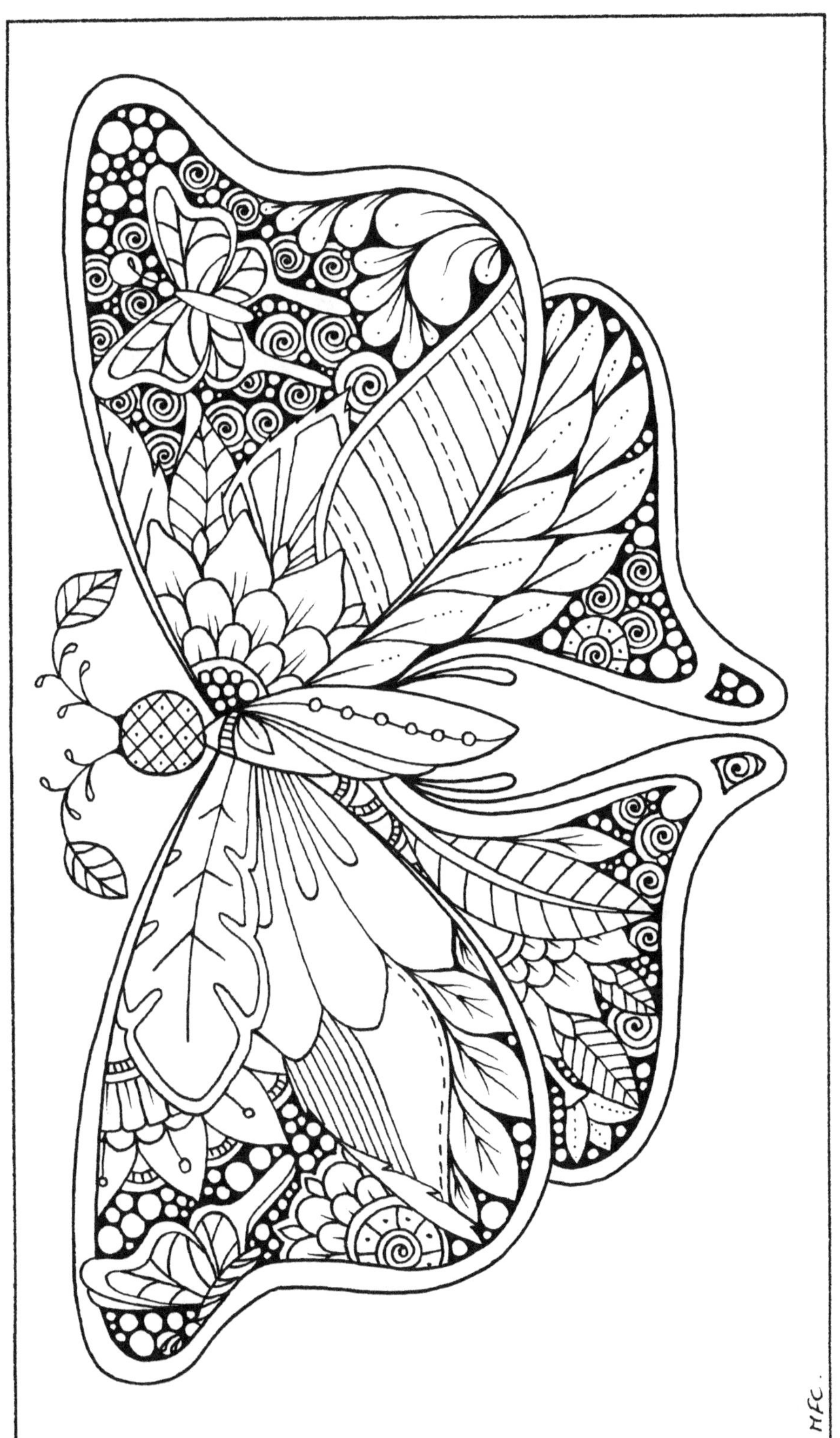

# Maud FERAL CHAUVEAU - (MFC)

## Enchanted Menagerie

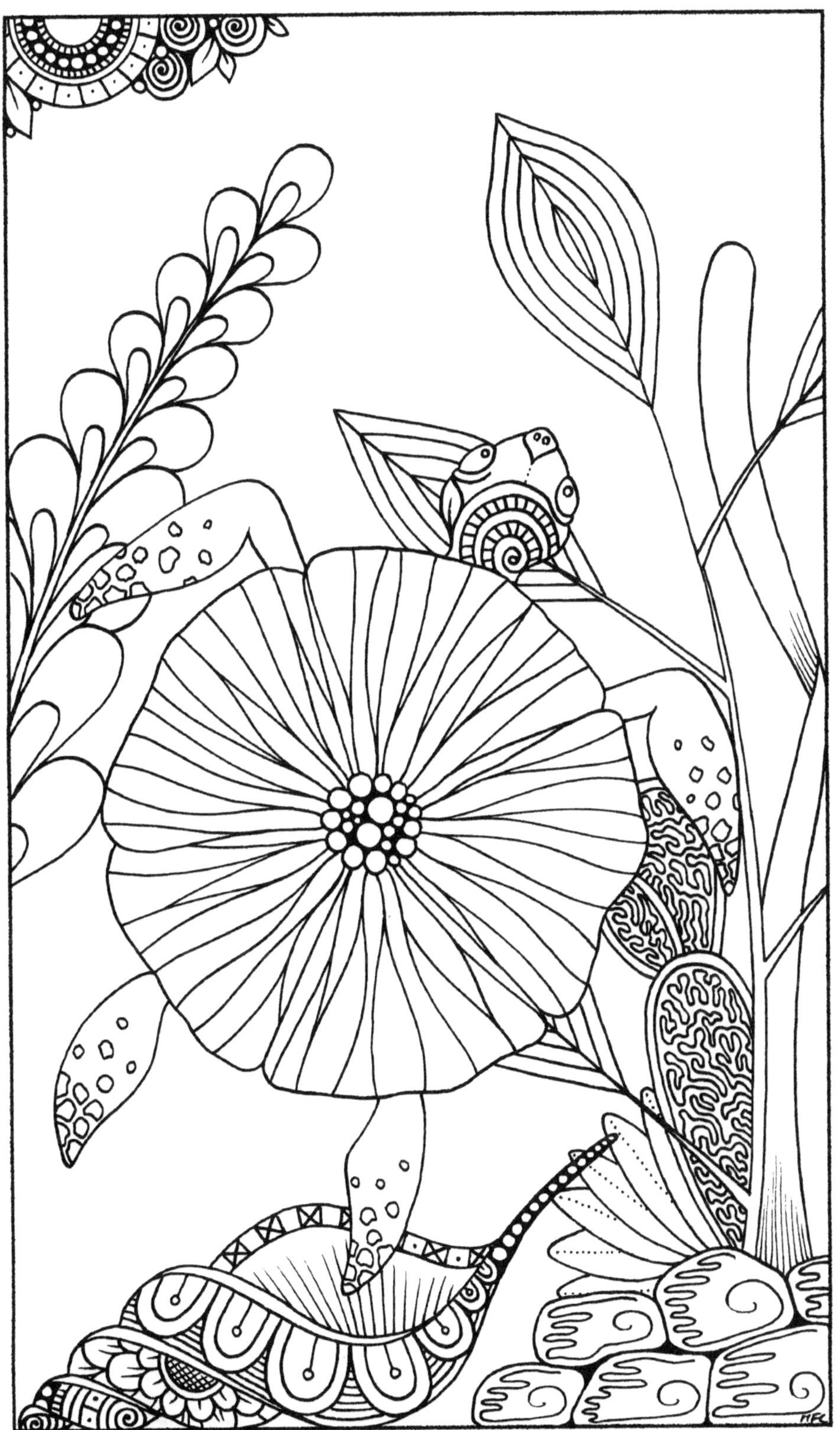

Maud FERAL CHAUVEAU - (MFC)

Enchanted Menagerie

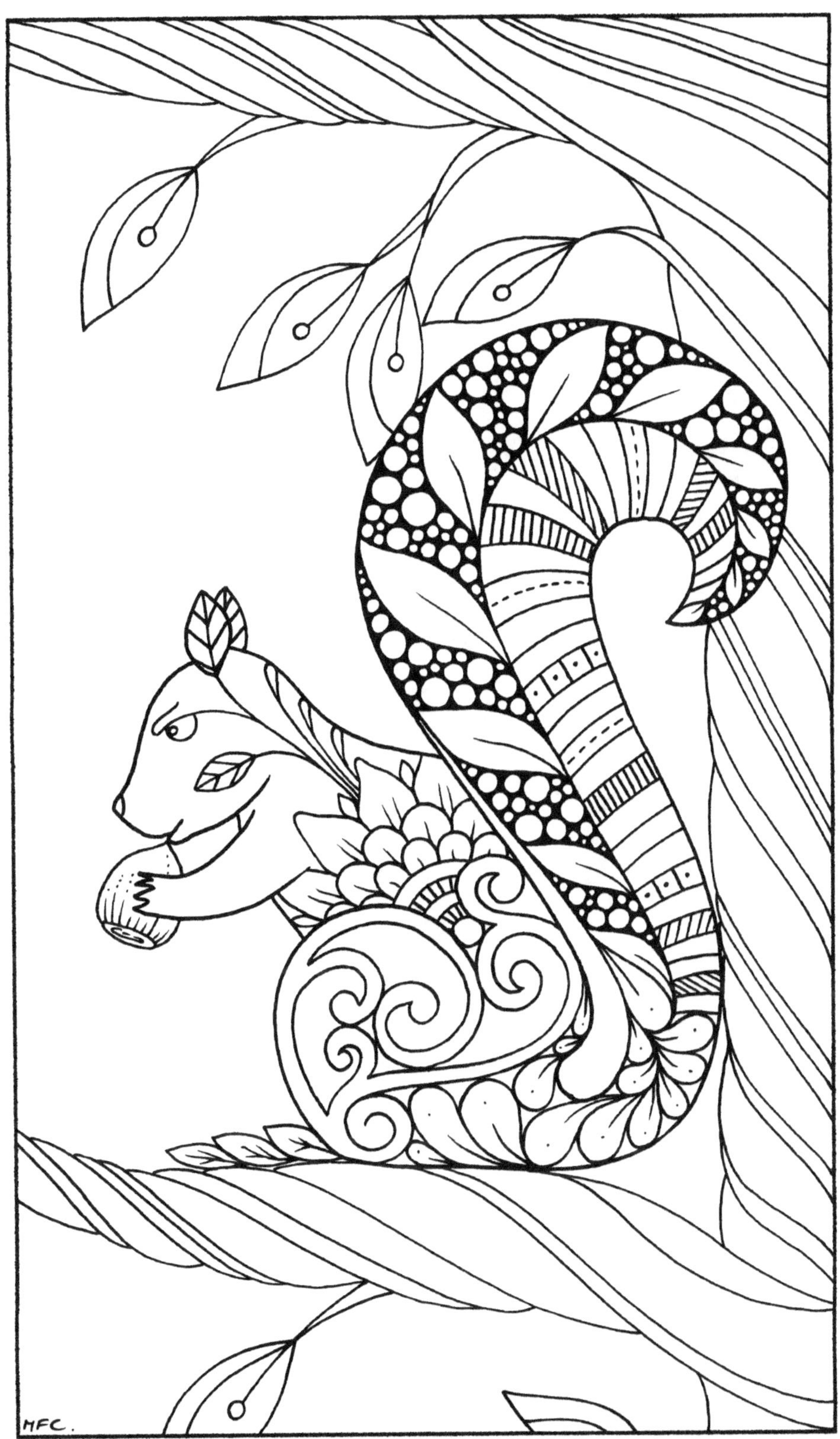
MFC.

# Maud FERAL CHAUVEAU - (MFC)

## Enchanted Menagerie

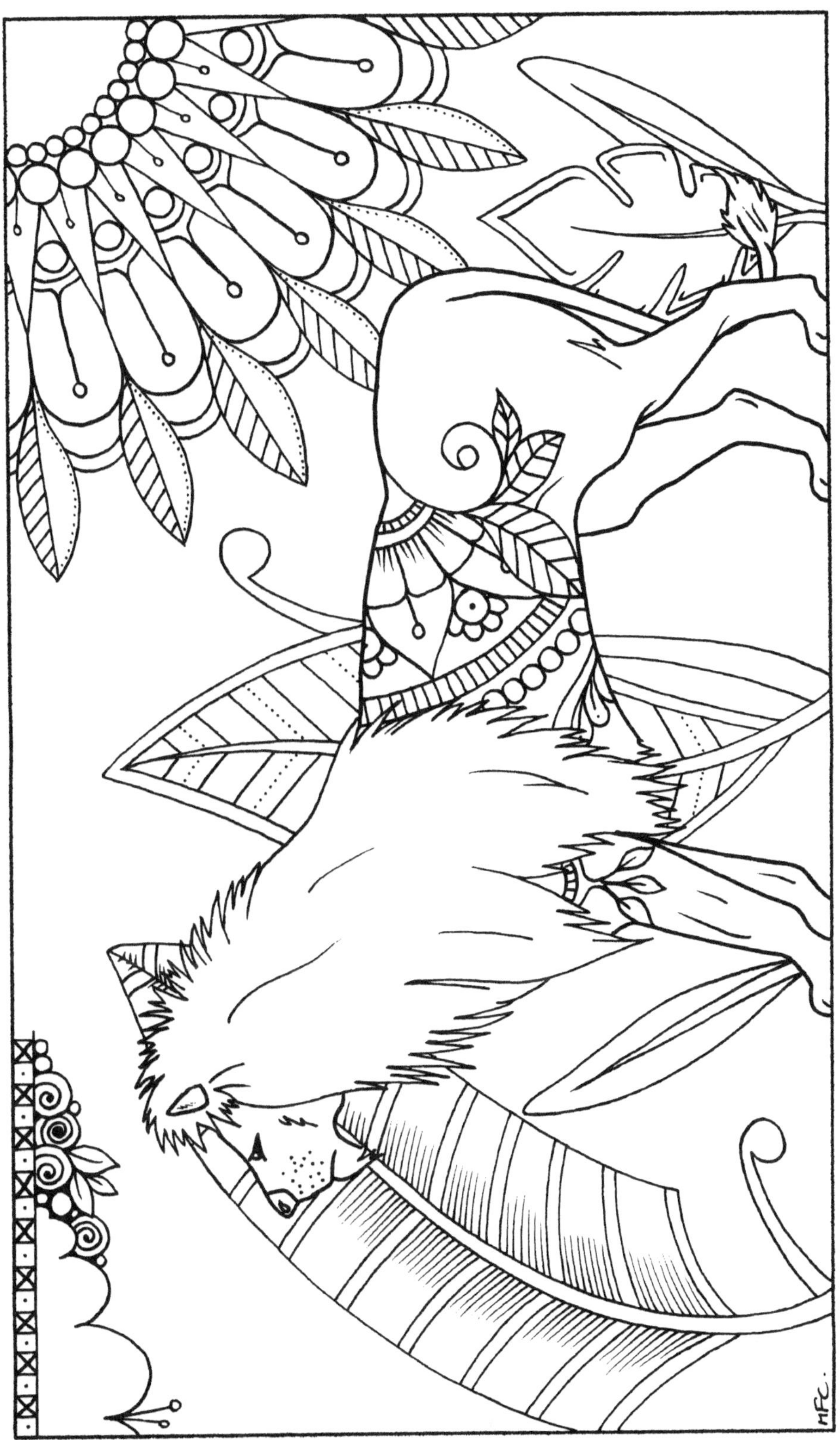

# Maud FERAL CHAUVEAU - (MFC)

## Enchanted Menagerie

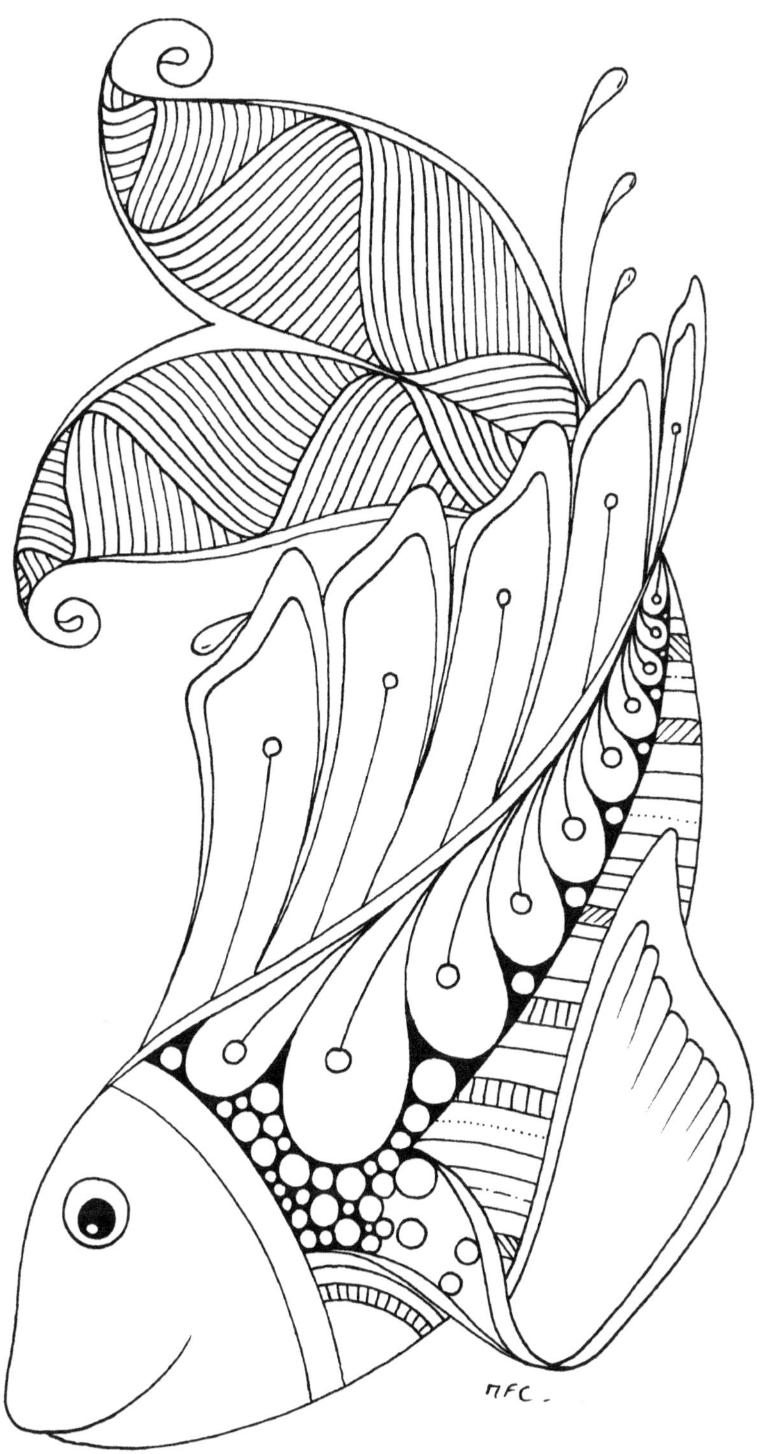

# Maud FERAL CHAUVEAU - (MFC)

## Enchanted Menagerie

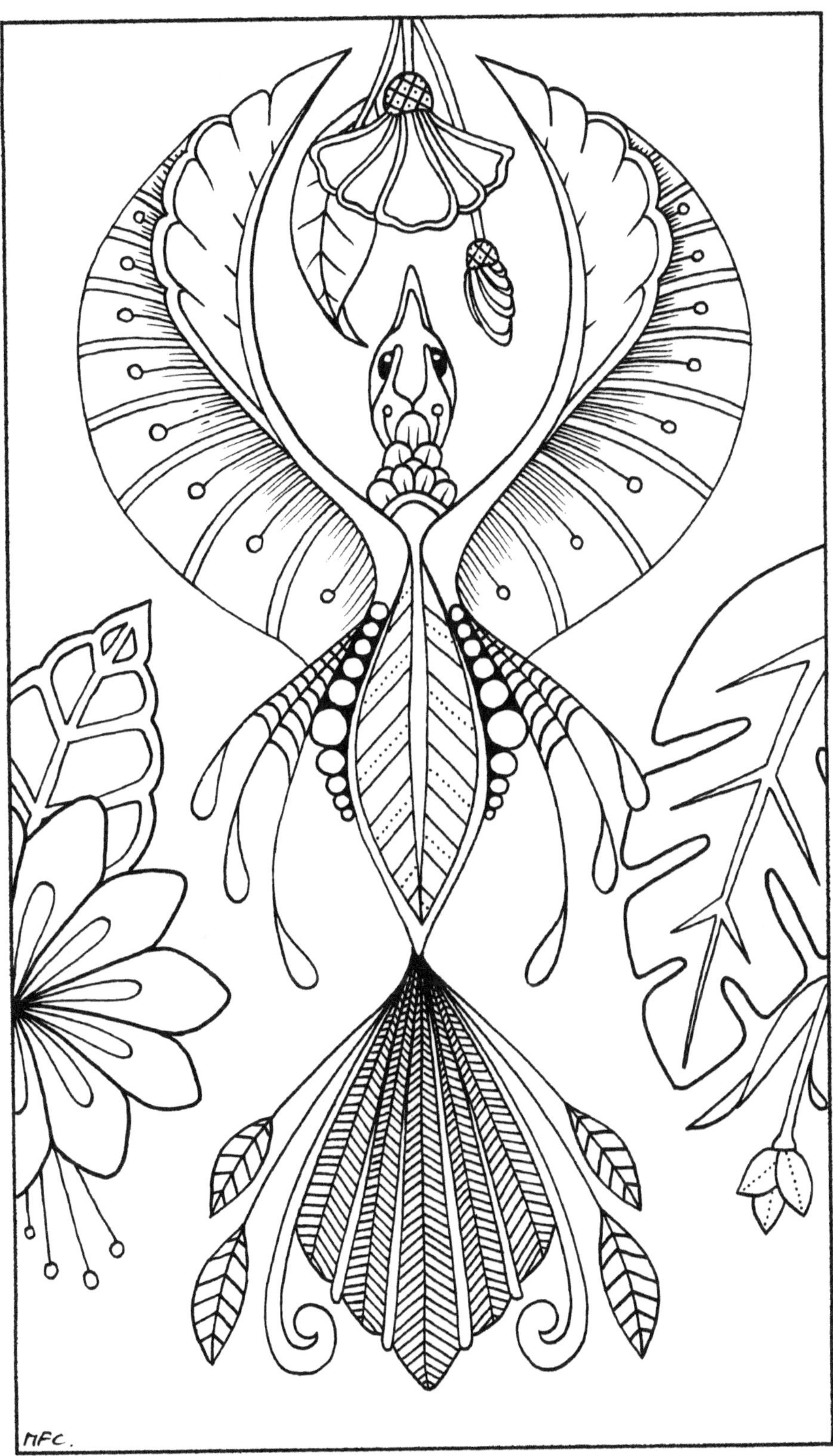
MFC.

# Maud FERAL CHAUVEAU - (MFC)

## Enchanted Menagerie

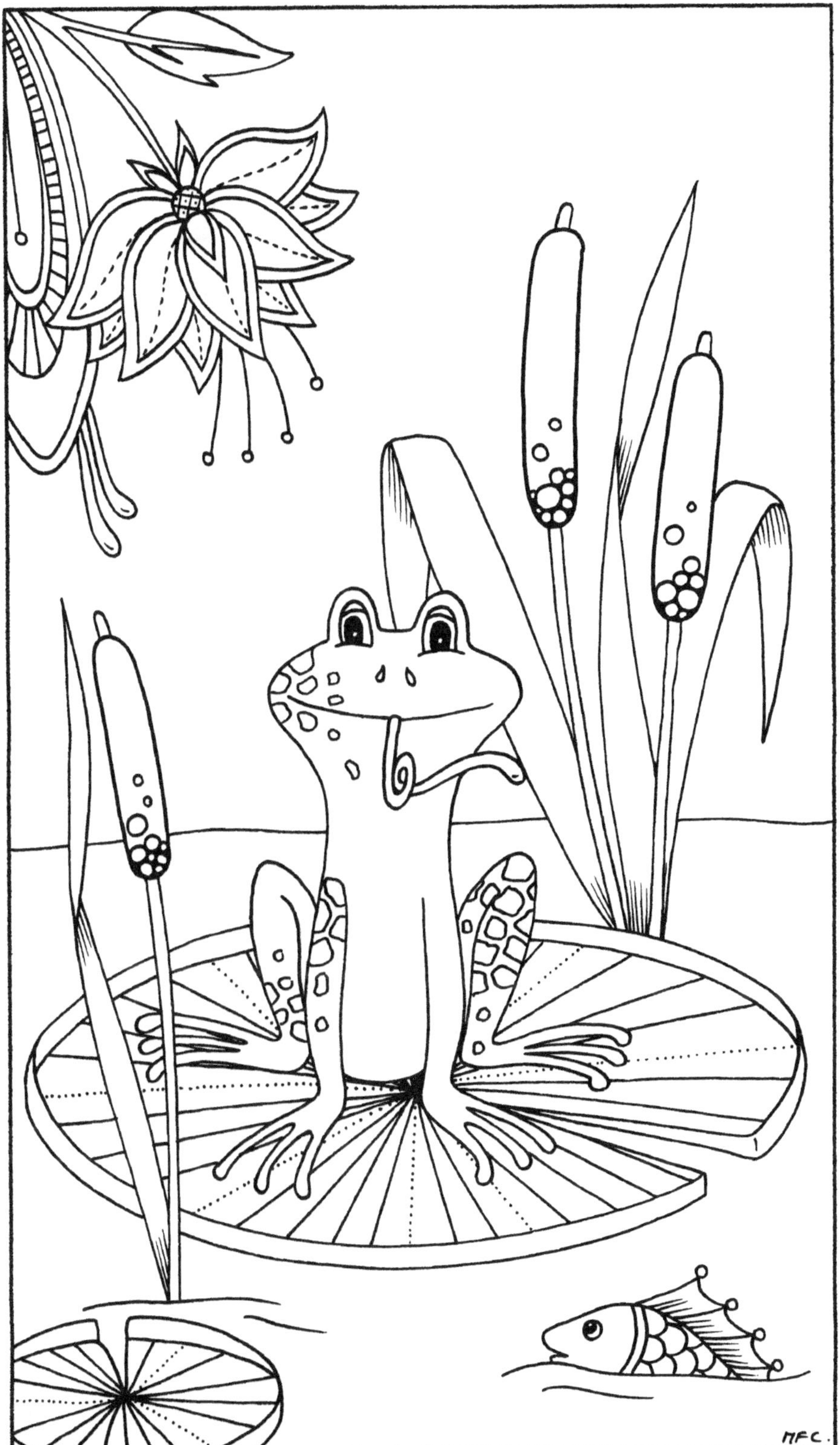
MFC.

Maud FERAL CHAUVEAU - (MFC)

Enchanted Menagerie

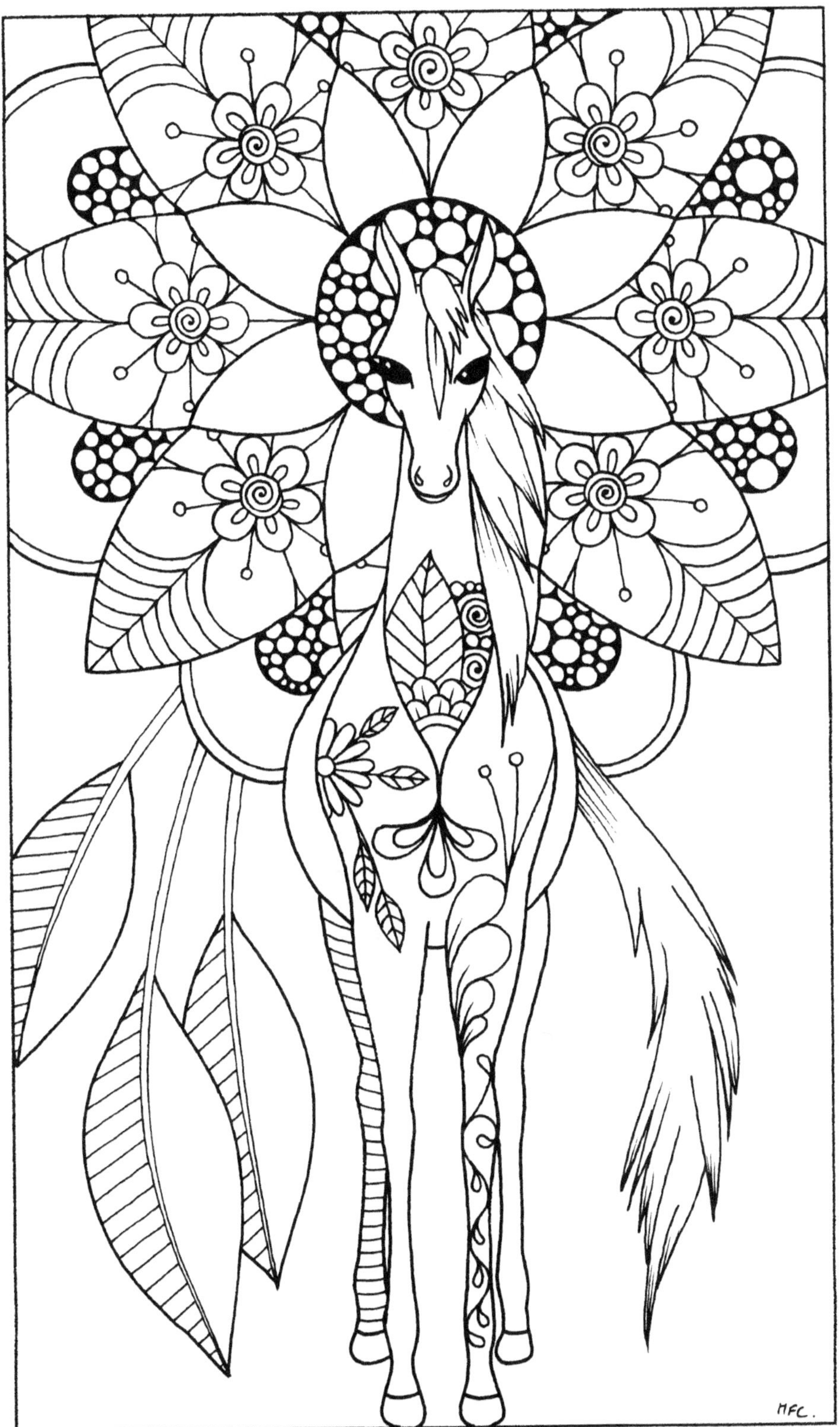
MFC.

Maud FERAL CHAUVEAU - (MFC)

Enchanted Menagerie

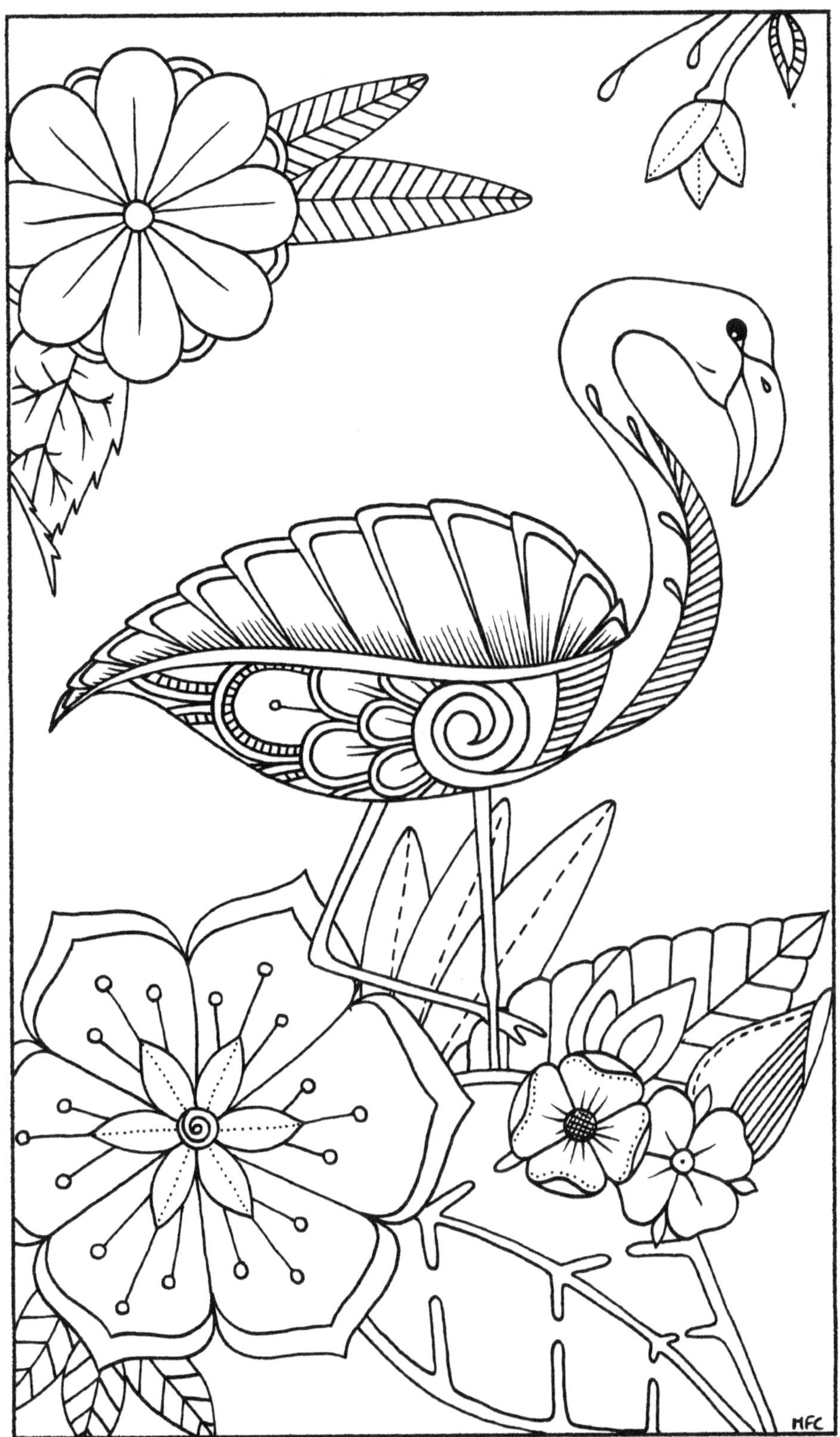

# Maud FERAL CHAUVEAU - (MFC)

## Enchanted Menagerie

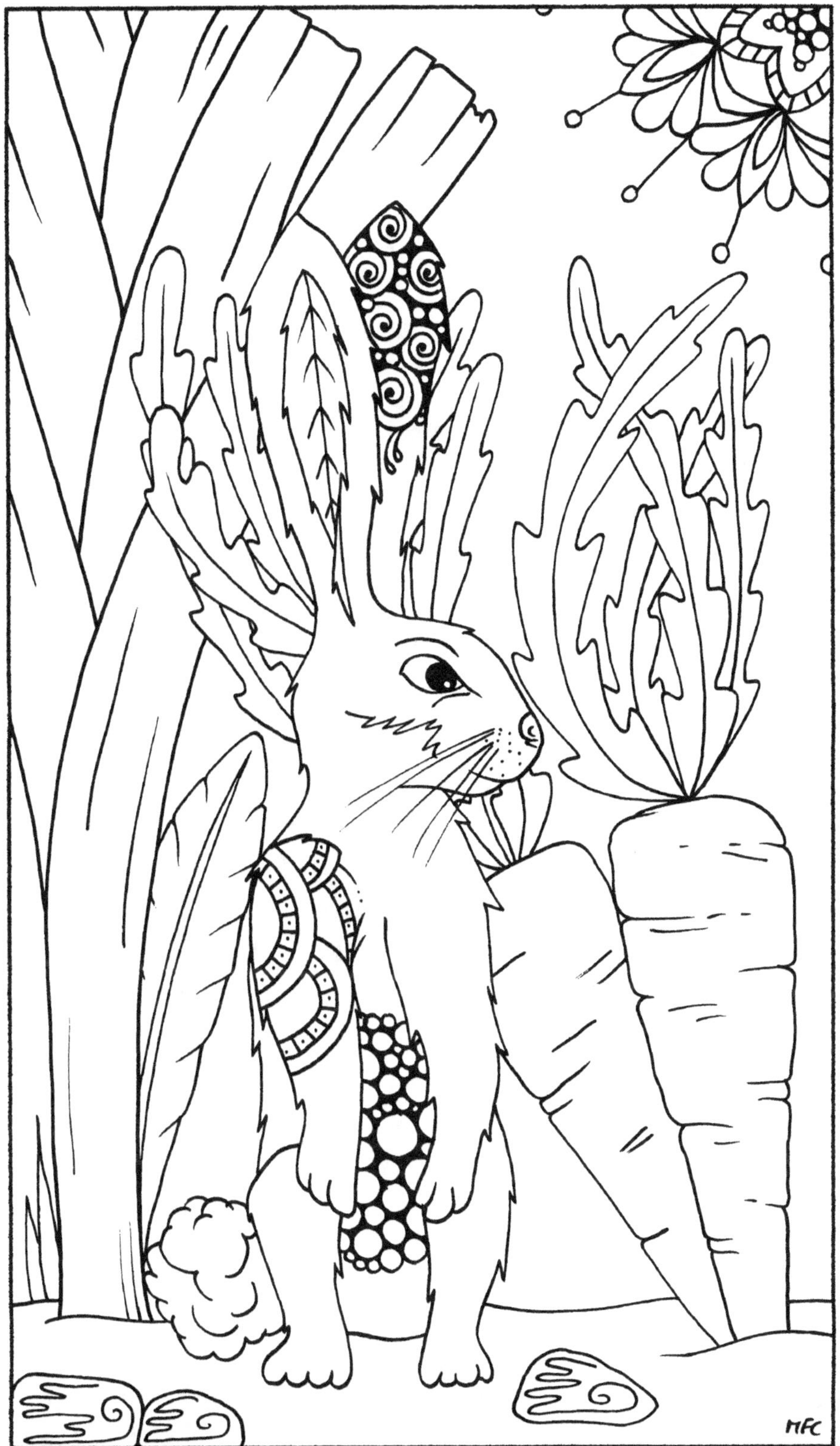
MFC

Maud FERAL CHAUVEAU - (MFC)

Enchanted Menagerie

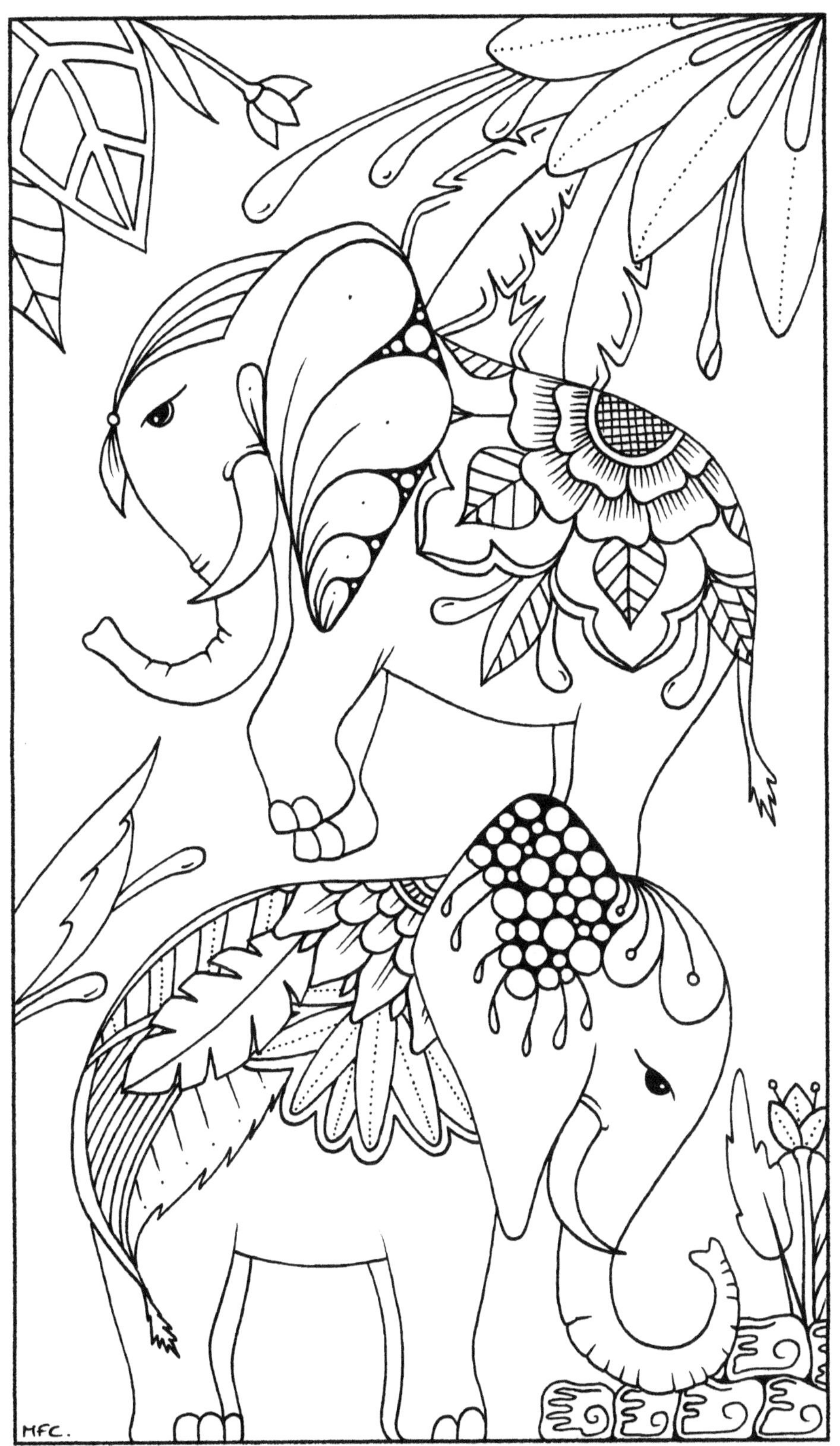
MFC.

# Maud FERAL CHAUVEAU - (MFC)

## Enchanted Menagerie

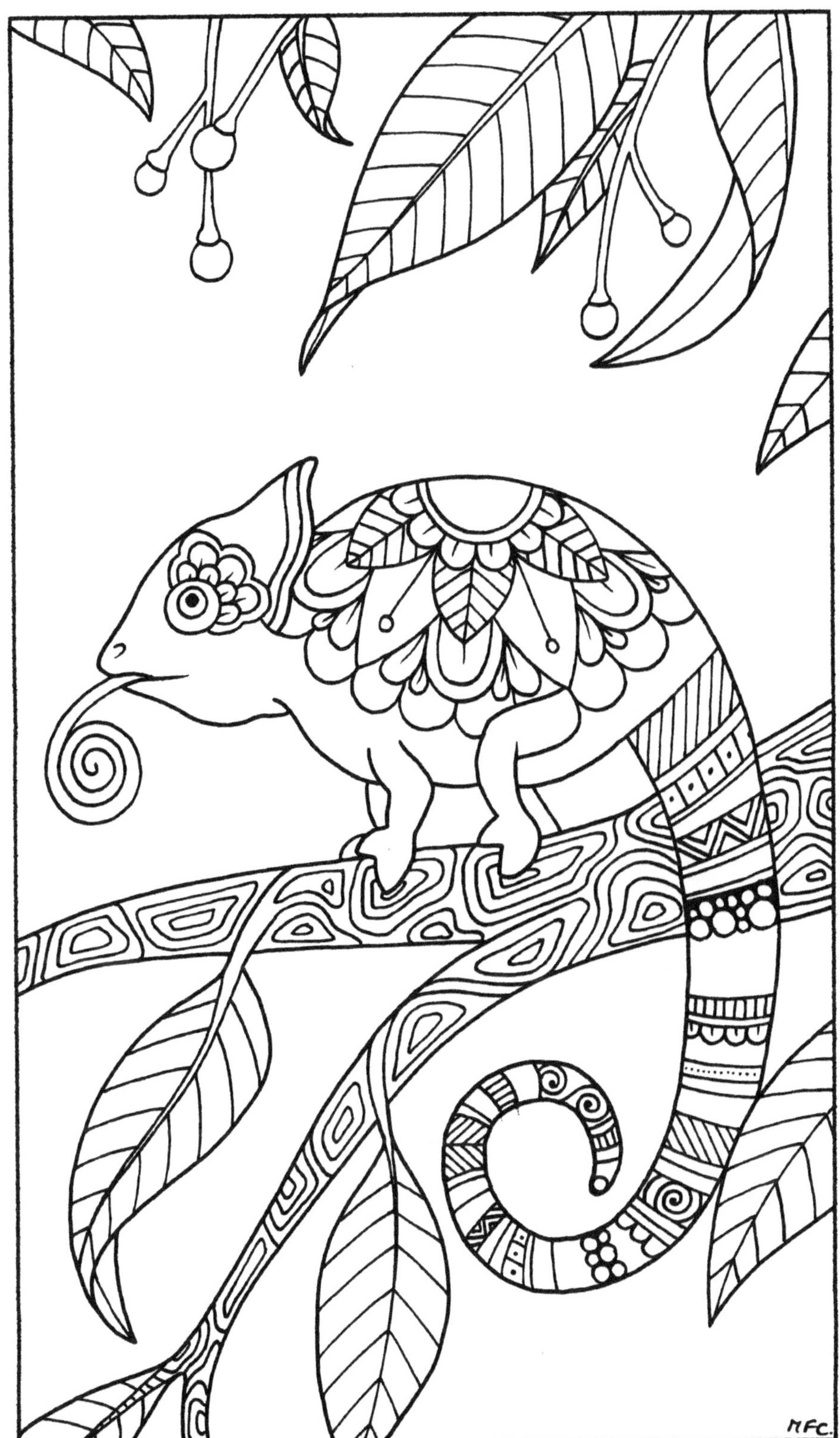

Maud FERAL CHAUVEAU - (MFC)

Enchanted Menagerie

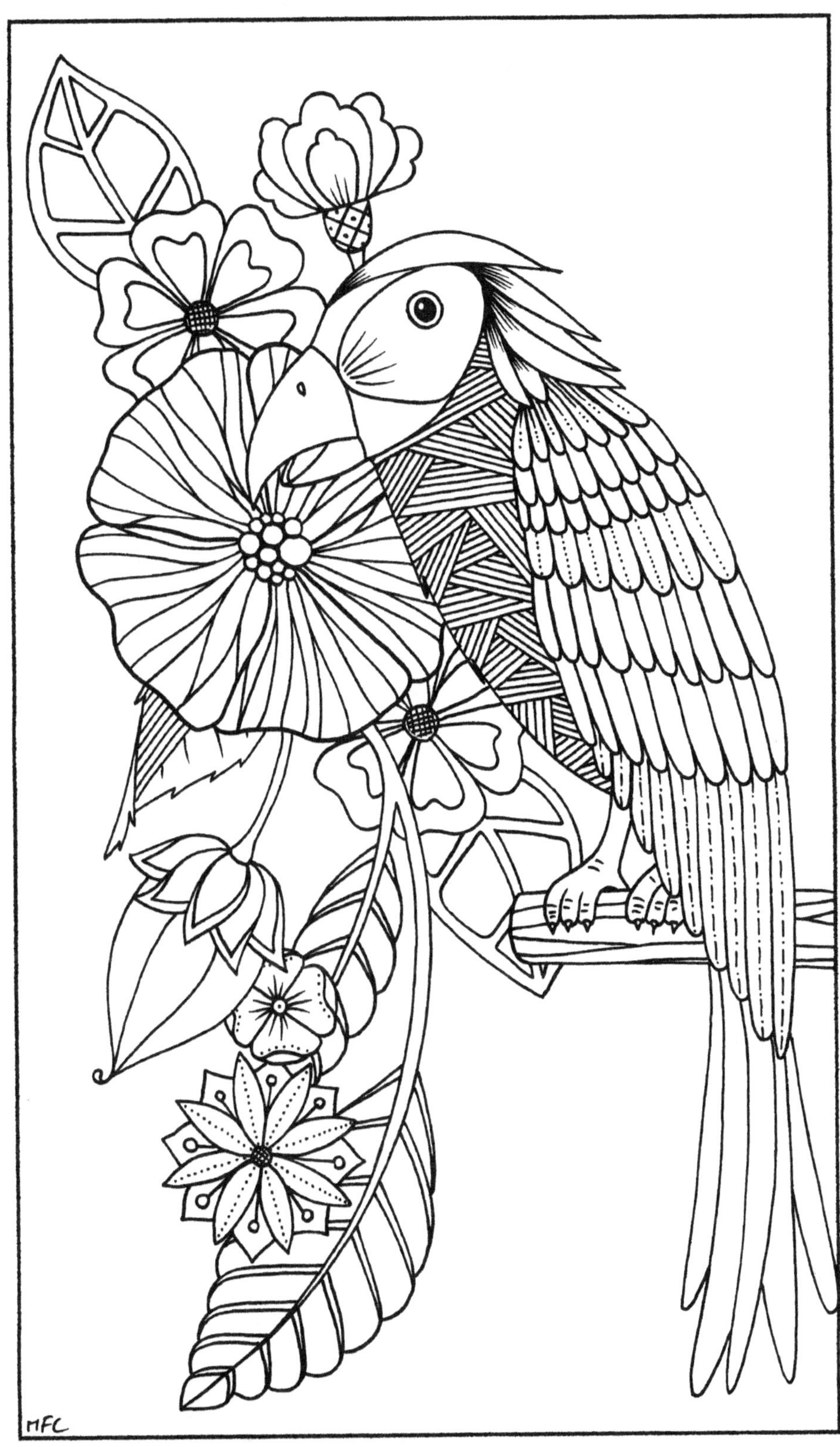
MFC

# Maud FERAL CHAUVEAU - (MFC)

## Enchanted Menagerie

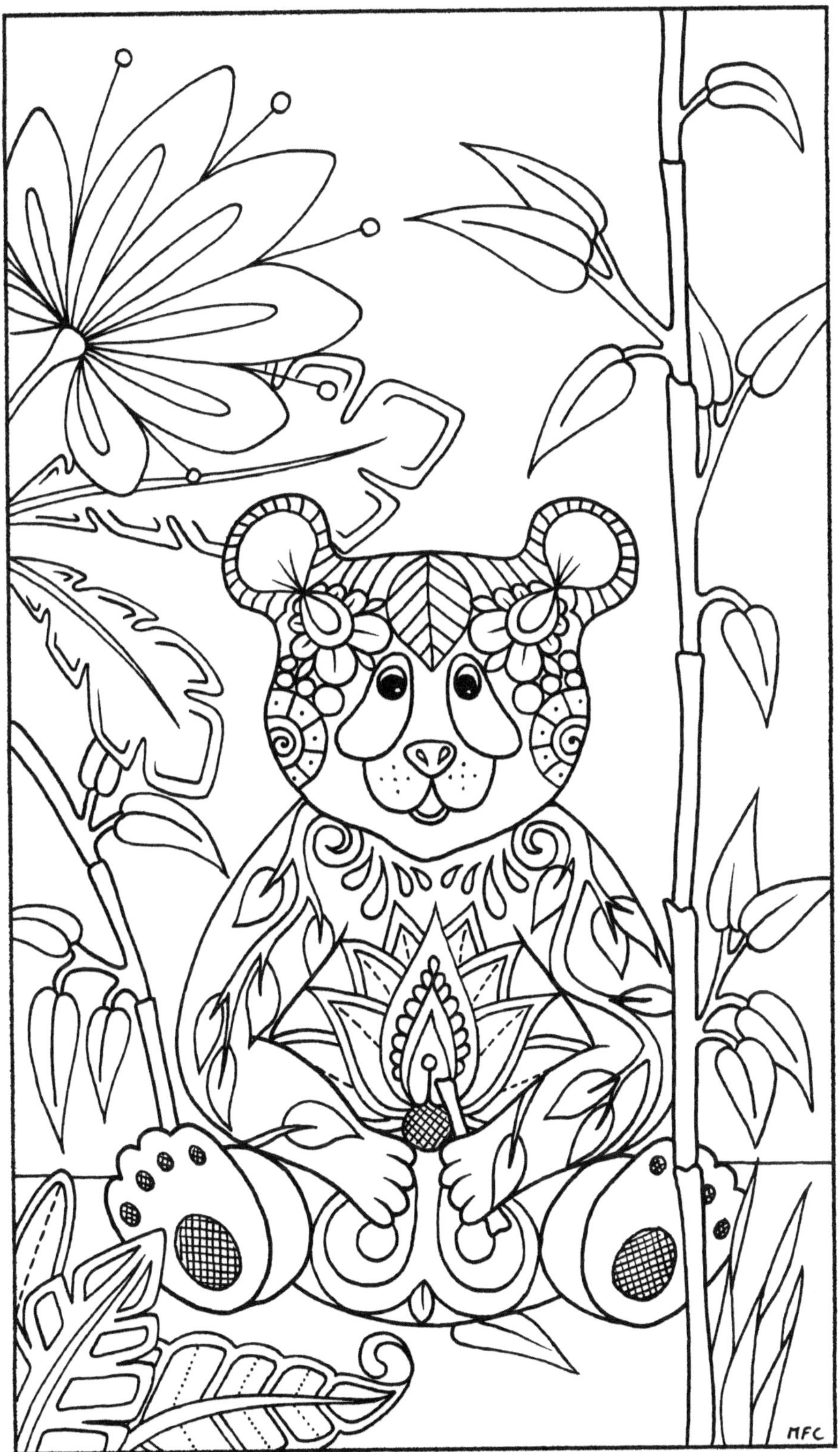

Maud FERAL CHAUVEAU - (MFC)

Enchanted Menagerie

Maud FERAL CHAUVEAU - (MFC)

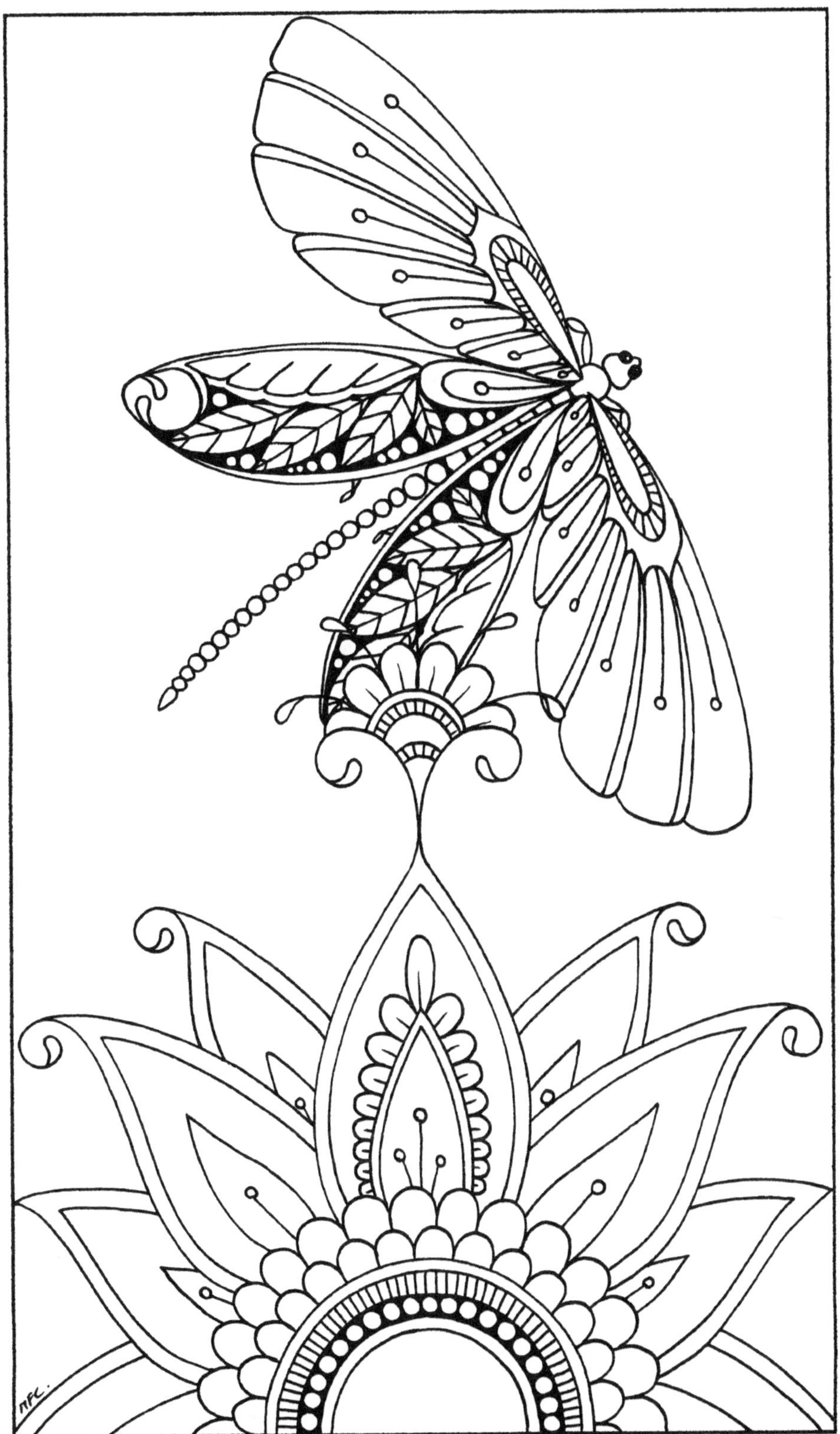

# Maud FERAL CHAUVEAU - (MFC)

## Enchanted Menagerie

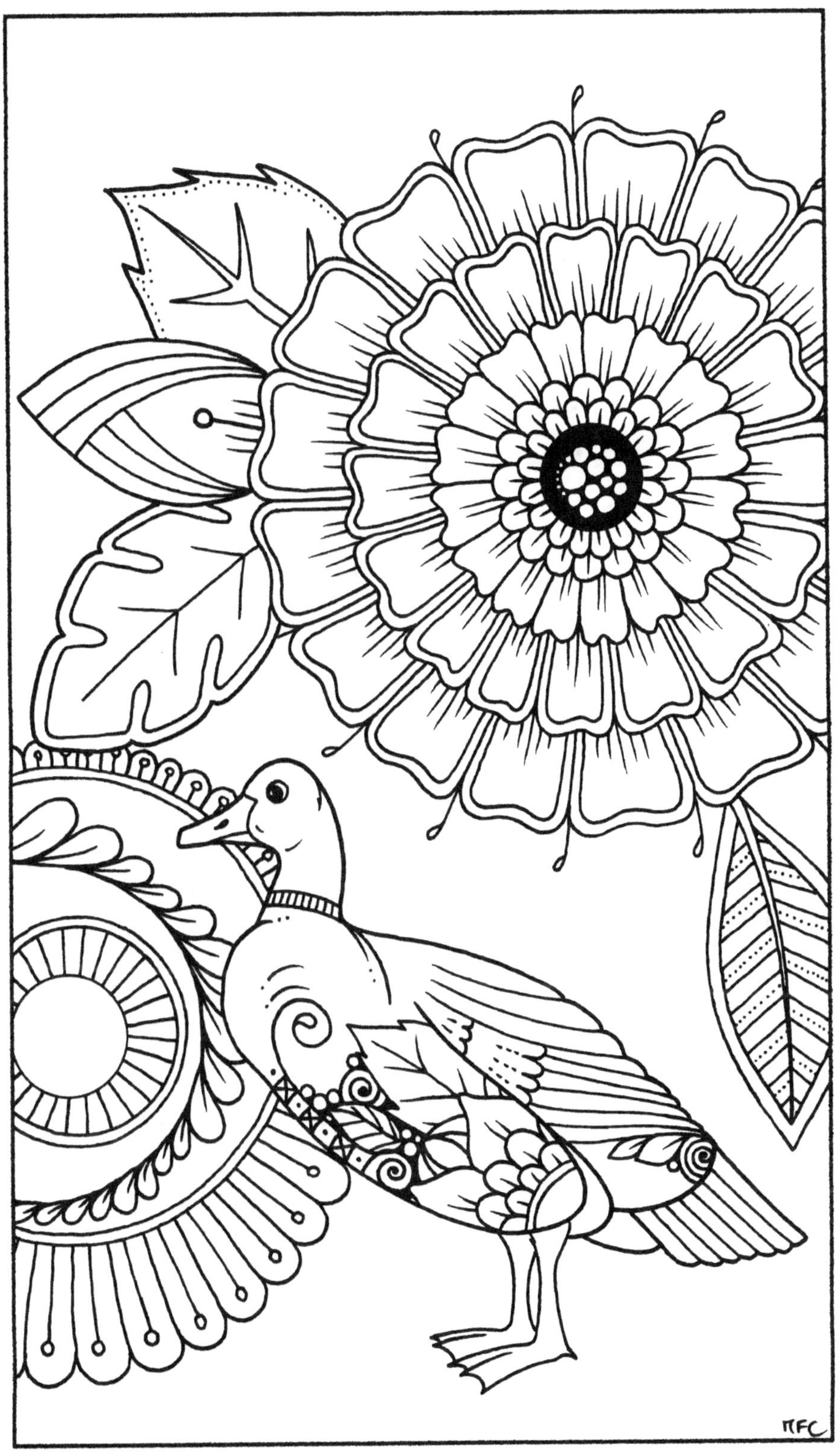

# Maud FERAL CHAUVEAU - (MFC)

## Enchanted Menagerie

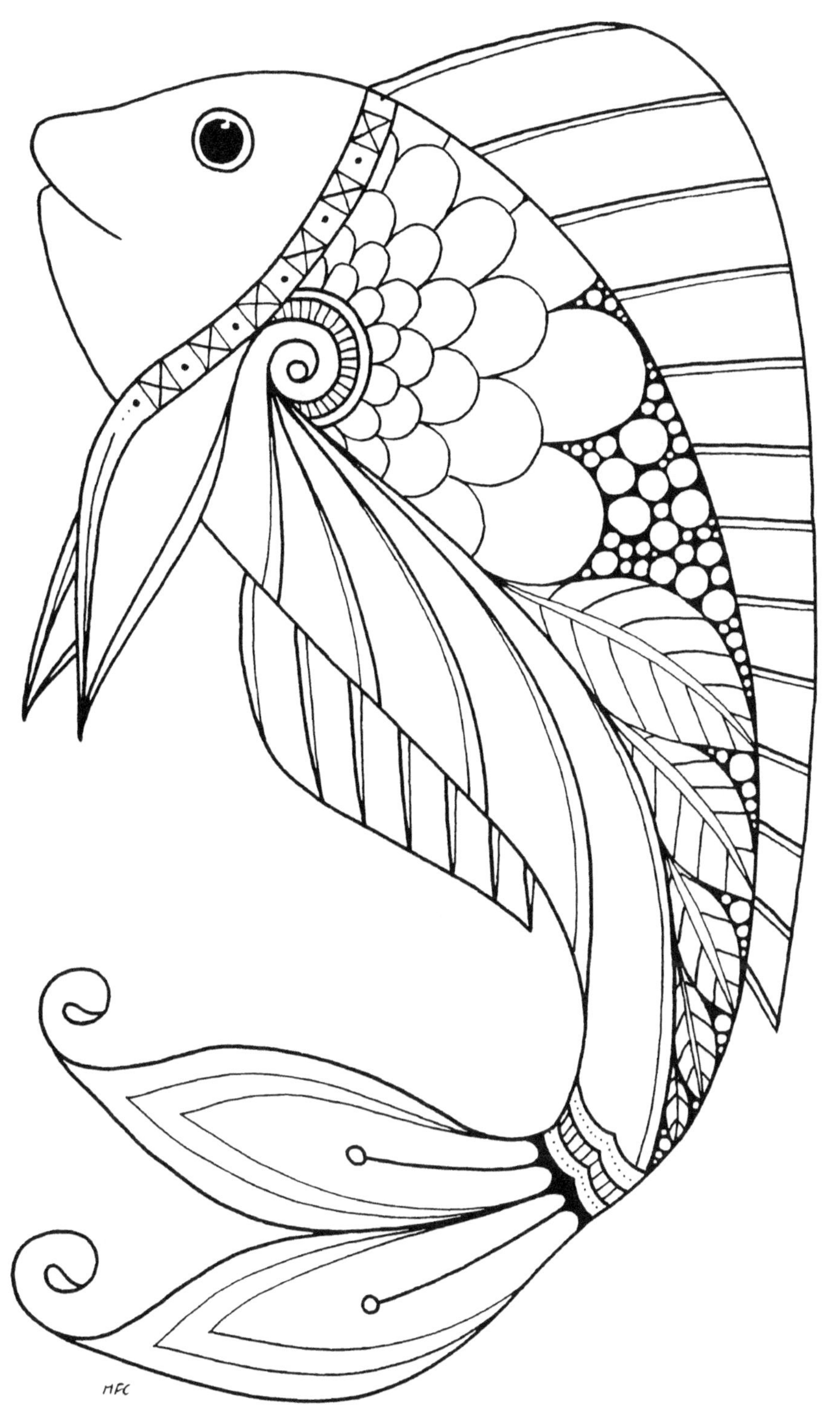

Maud FERAL CHAUVEAU - (MFC)

Enchanted Menagerie

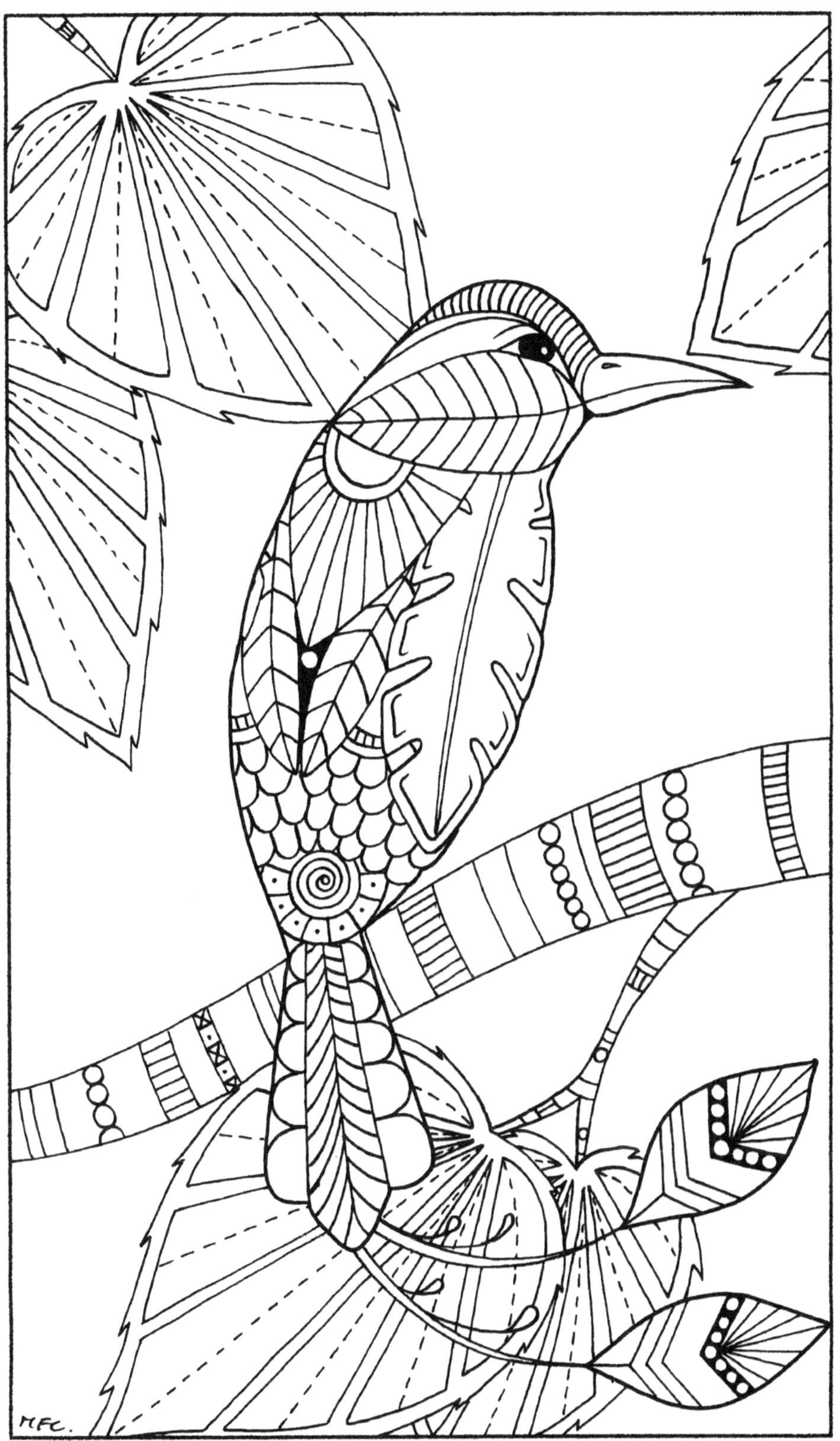
MFc.

# Maud FERAL CHAUVEAU - (MFC)

## Enchanted Menagerie

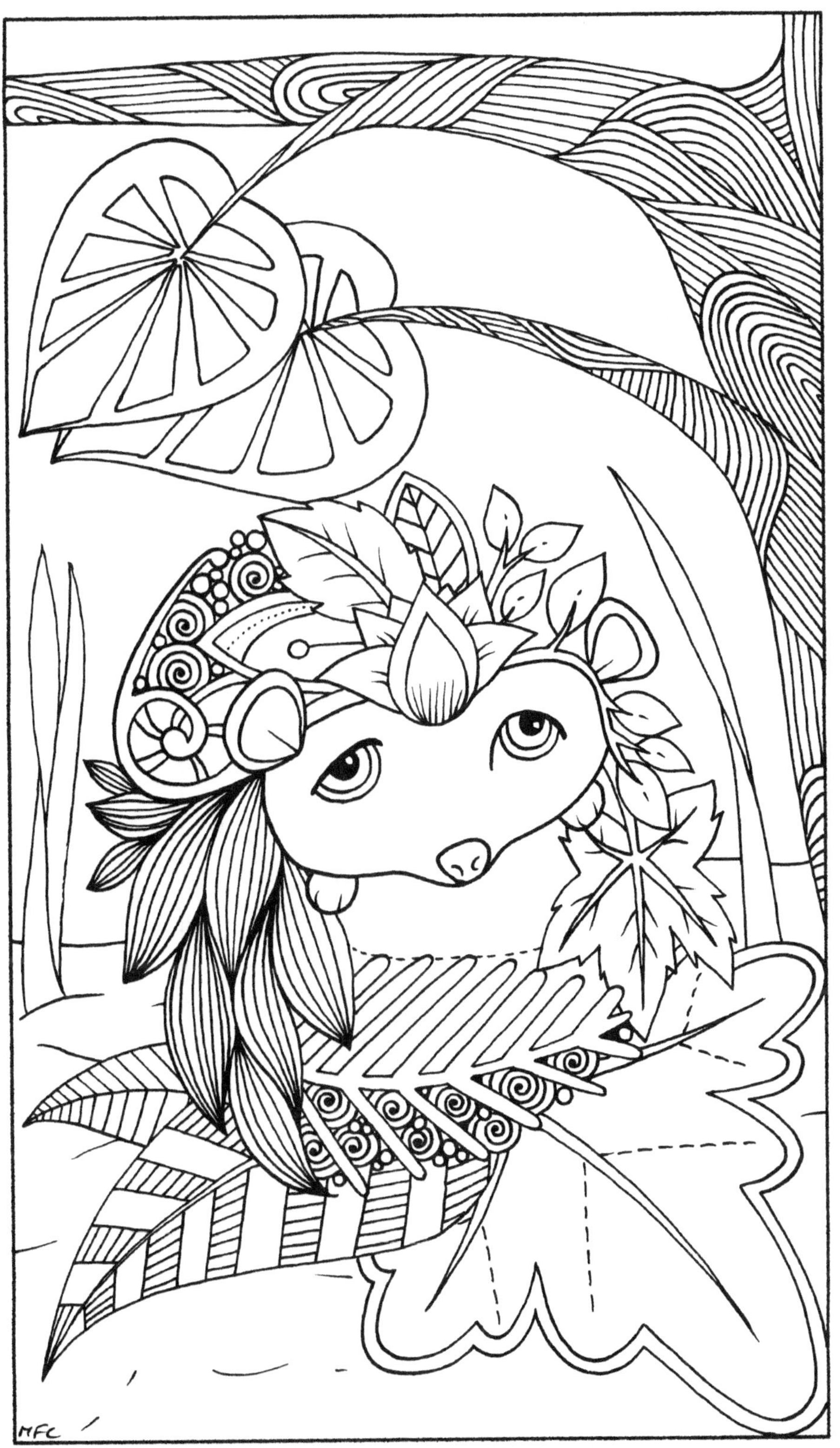
MFC

# Maud FERAL CHAUVEAU - (MFC)

## Enchanted Menagerie

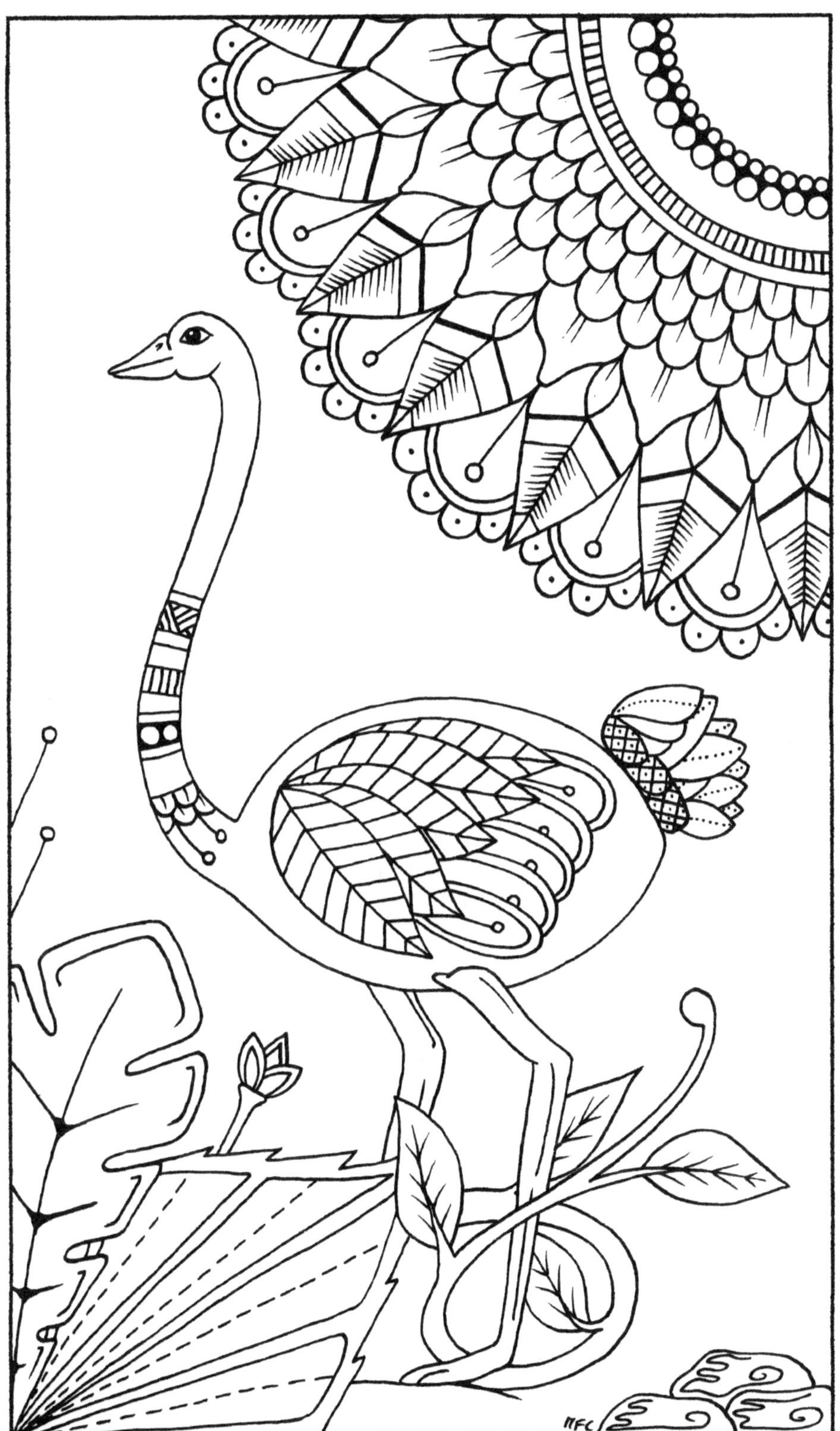

Maud FERAL CHAUVEAU - (MFC)

Enchanted Menagerie

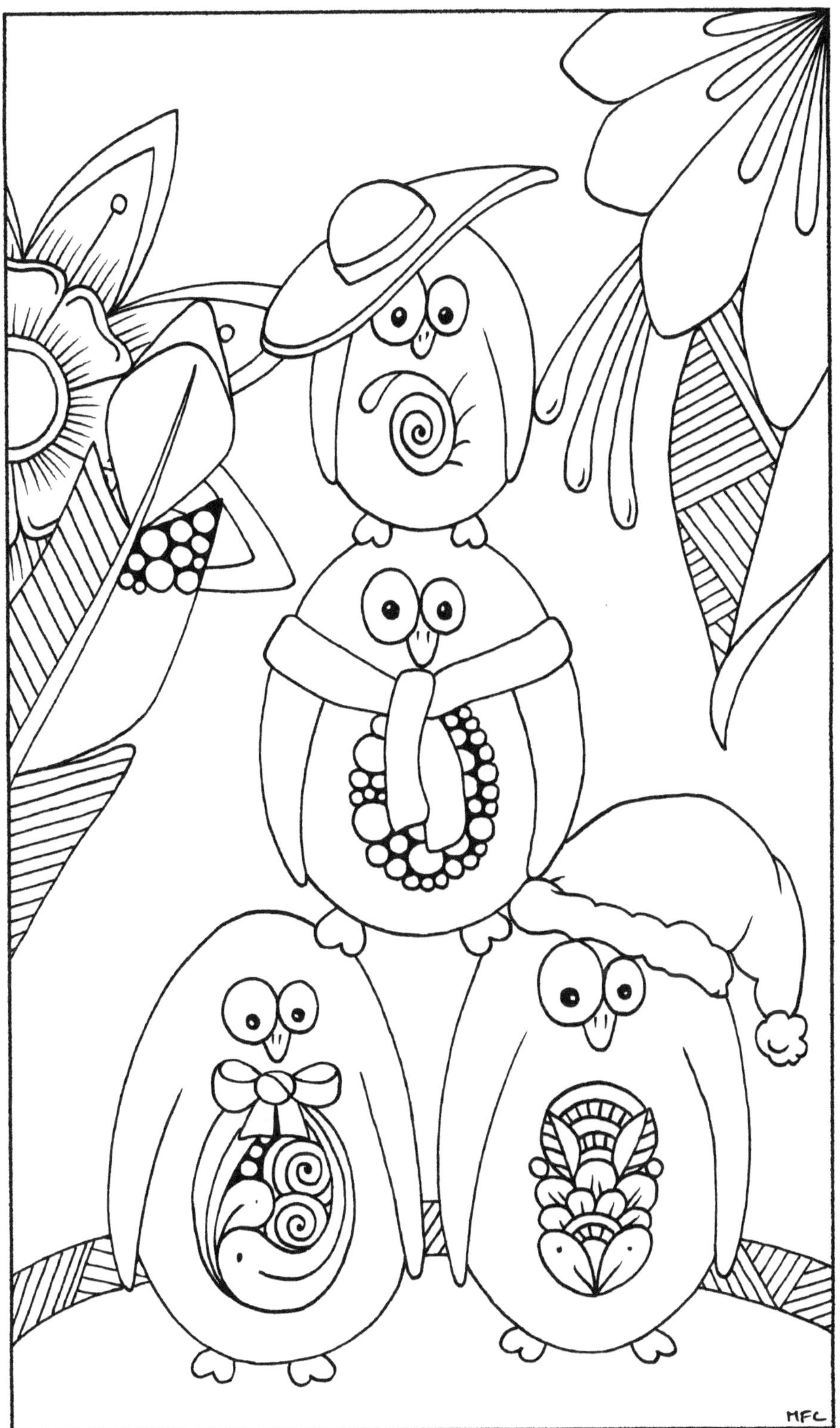

# Maud FERAL CHAUVEAU - (MFC)

## Enchanted Menagerie

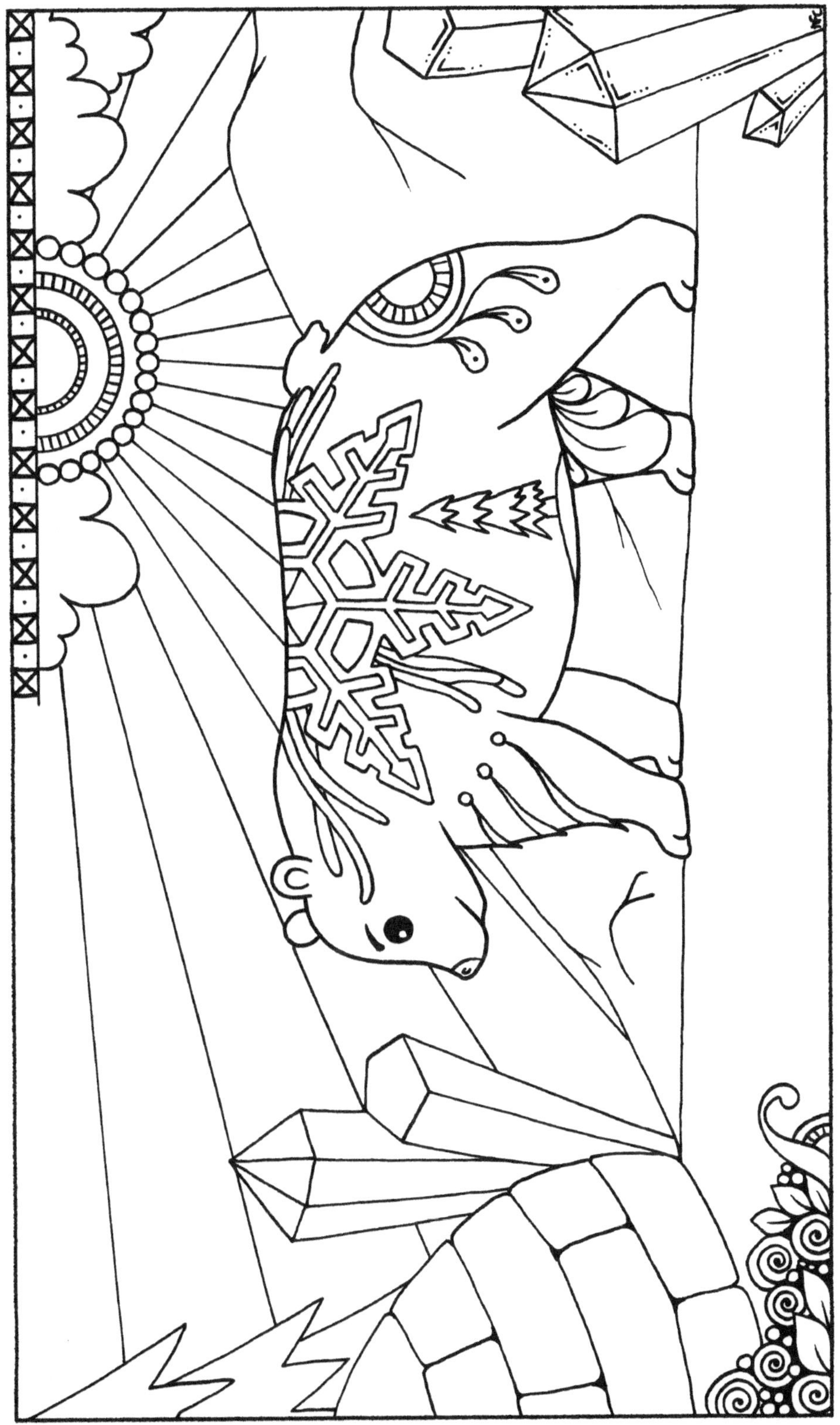

# Maud FERAL CHAUVEAU - (MFC)

## Enchanted Menagerie

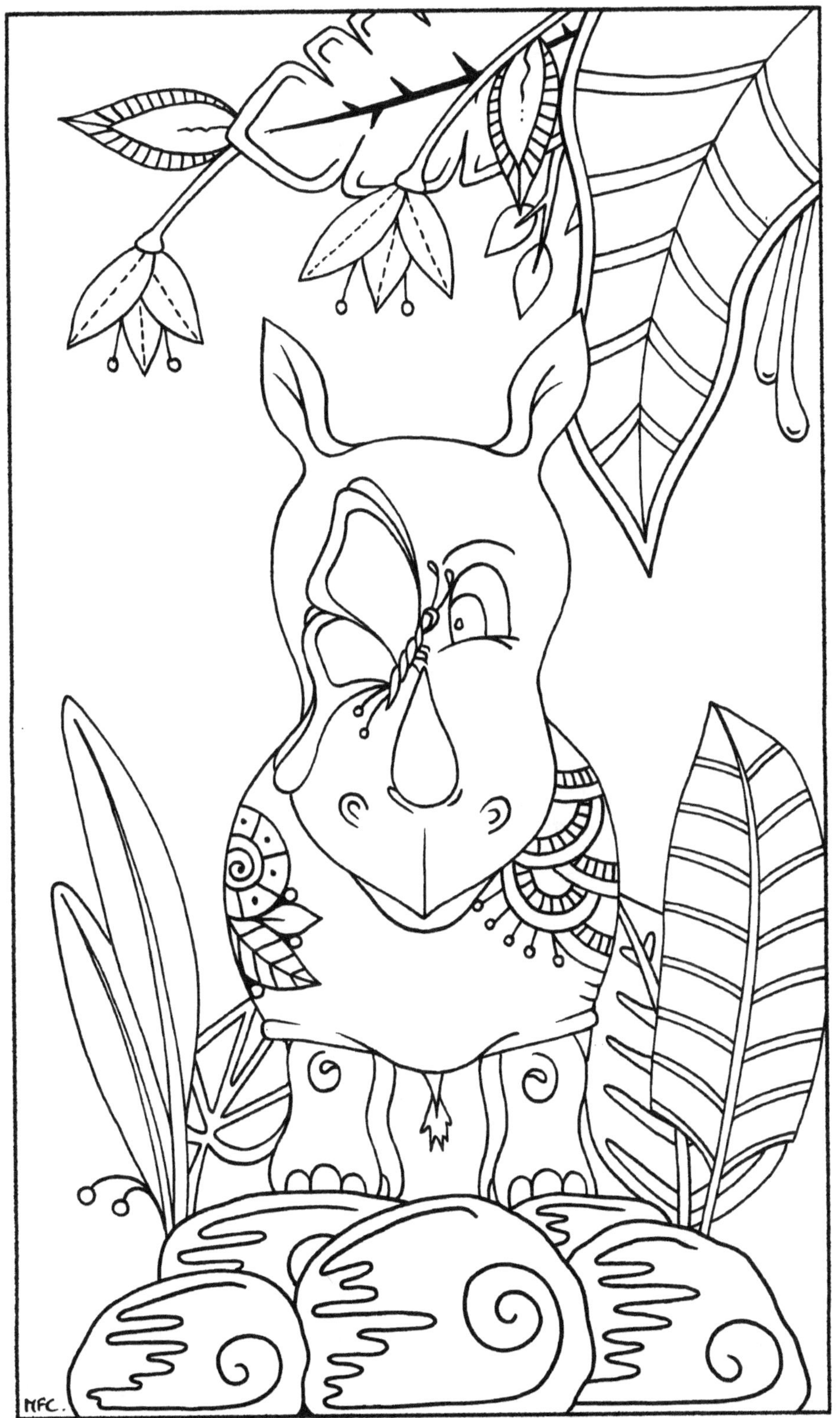
MFC.

Maud FERAL CHAUVEAU - (MFC)

Enchanted Menagerie

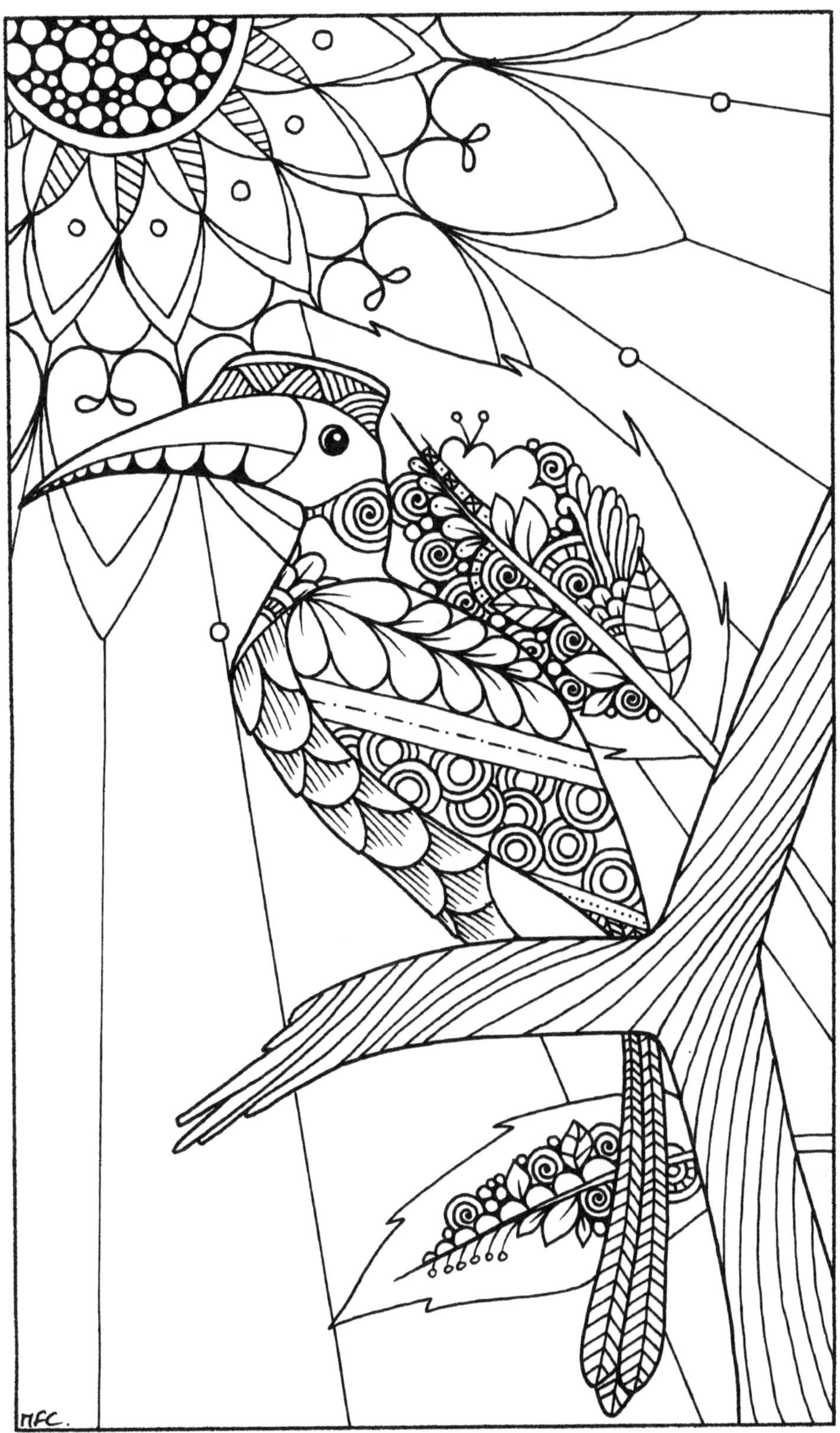
MFC.

# Maud FERAL CHAUVEAU - (MFC)

## Enchanted Menagerie

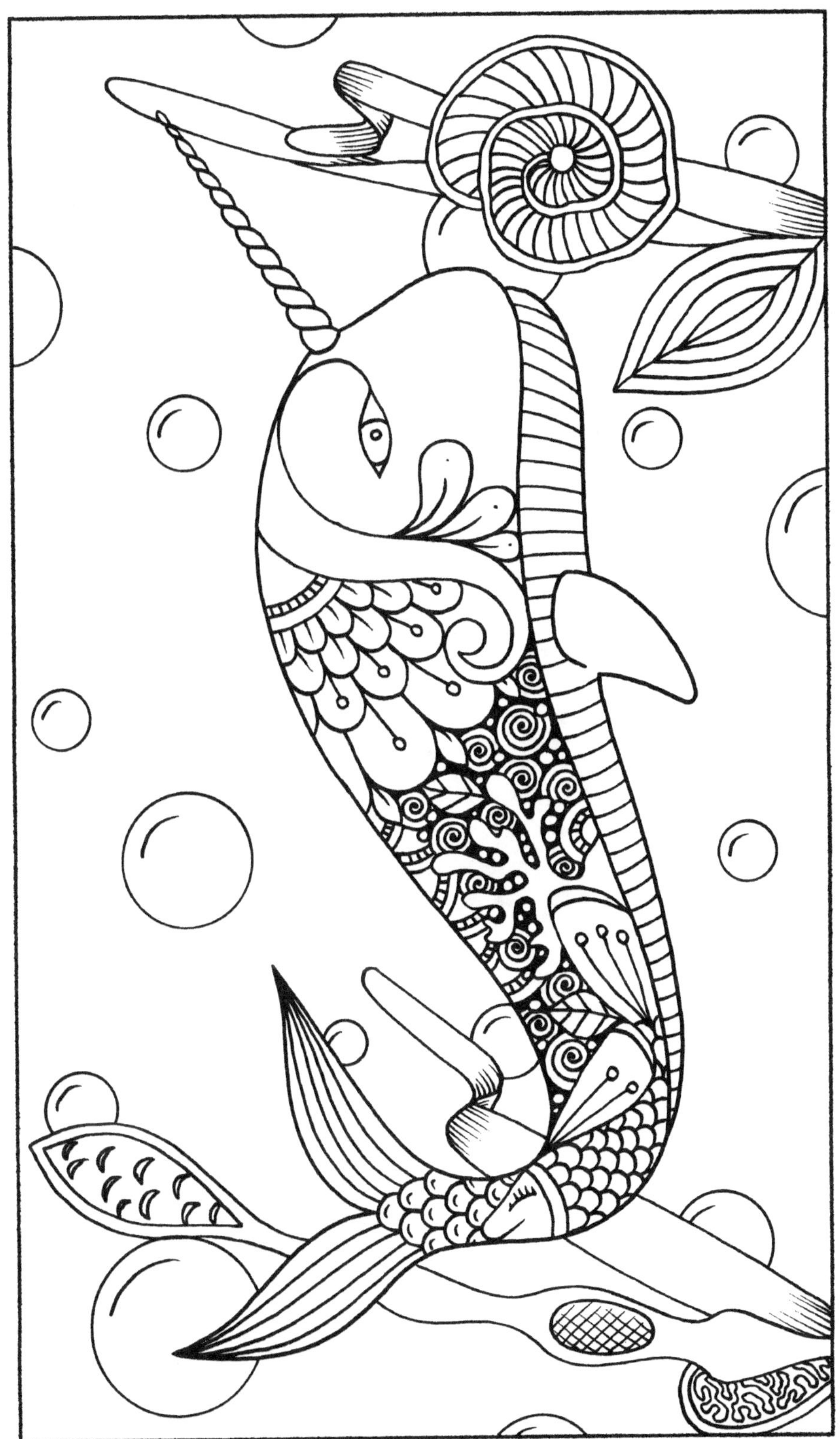

# Maud FERAL CHAUVEAU - (MFC)

## Enchanted Menagerie

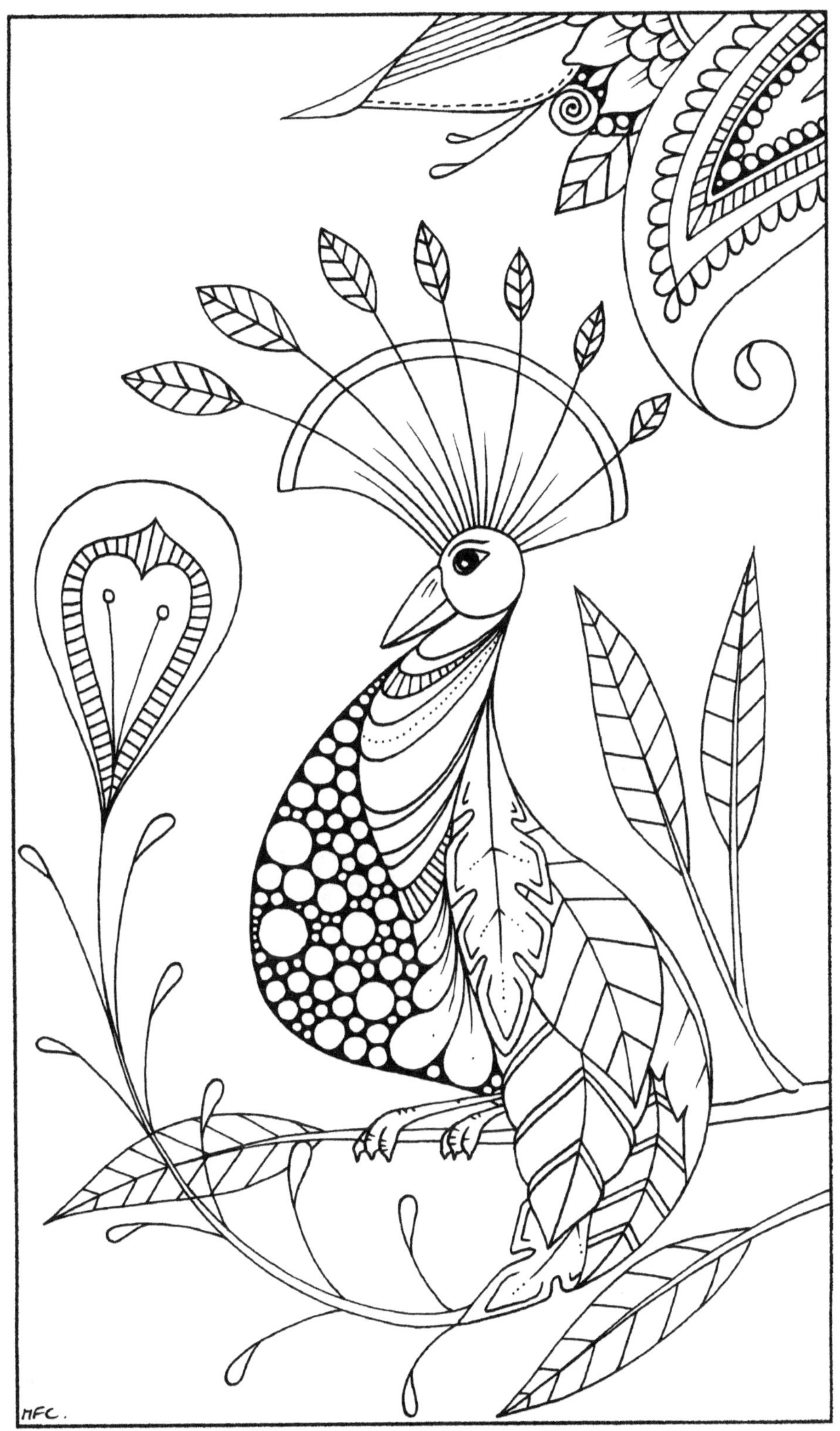

MFC.

# Maud FERAL CHAUVEAU - (MFC)

## Enchanted Menagerie

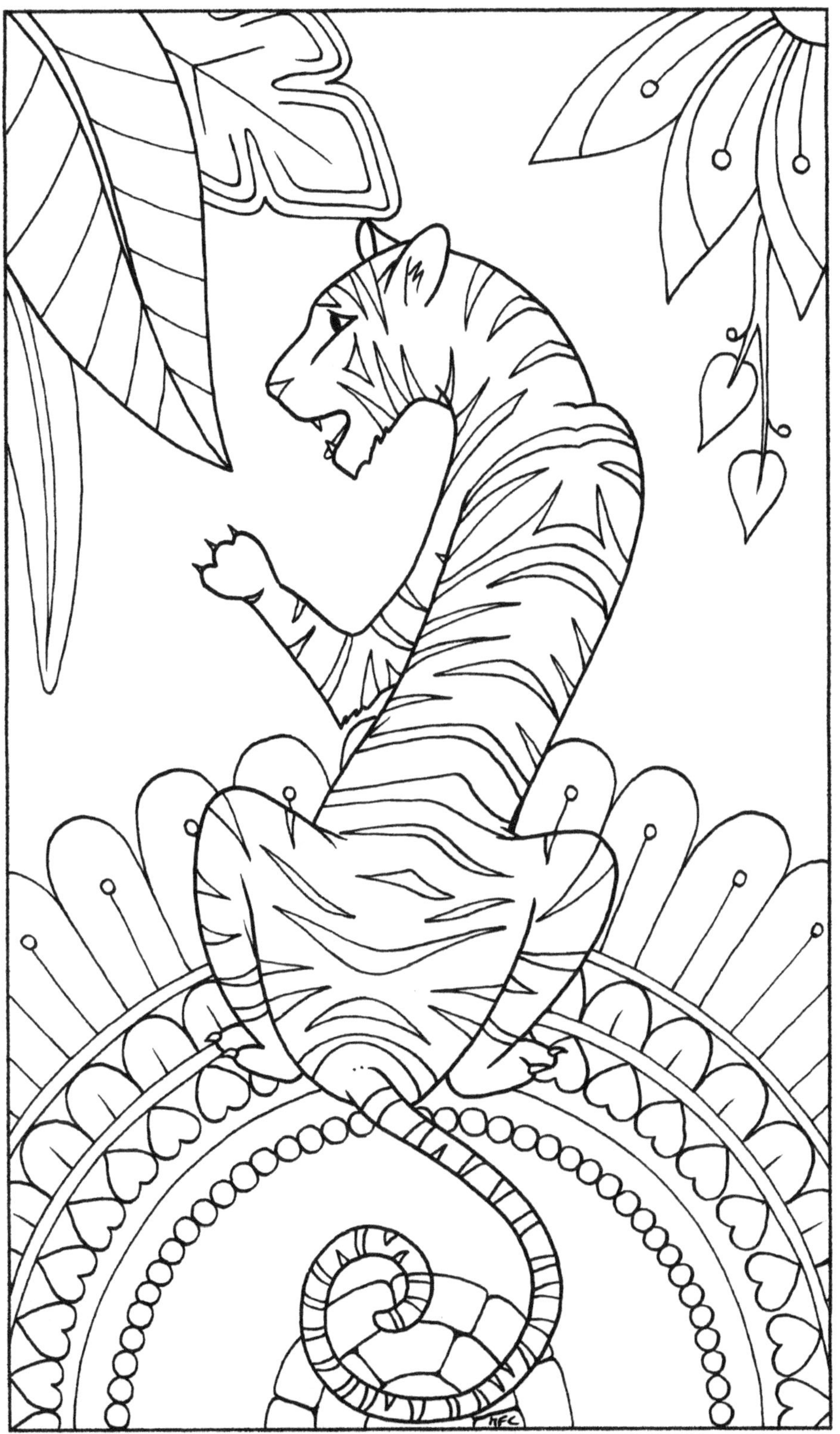

Maud FERAL CHAUVEAU - (MFC)

Enchanted Menagerie

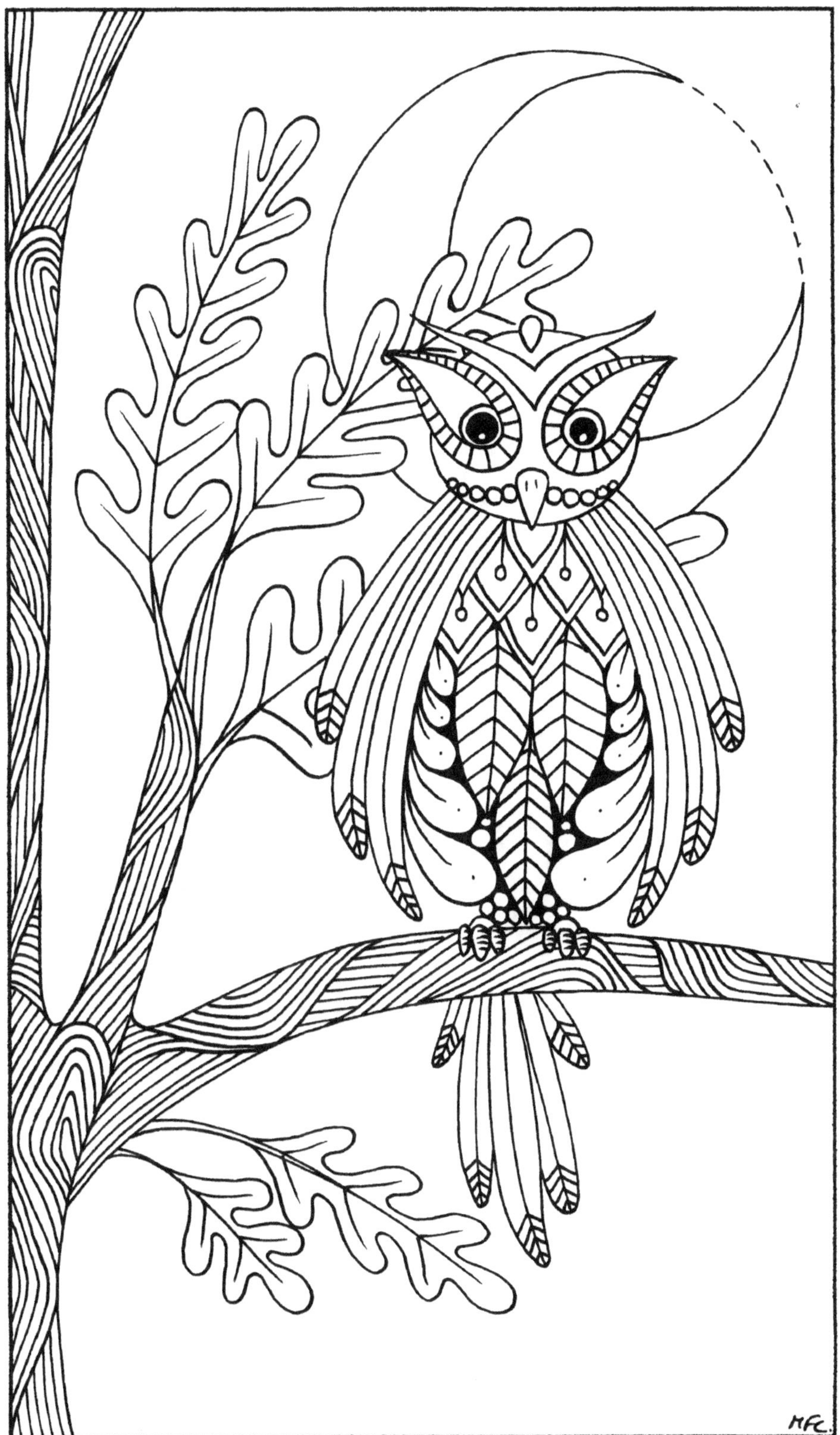

# Maud FERAL CHAUVEAU - (MFC)

## Enchanted Menagerie

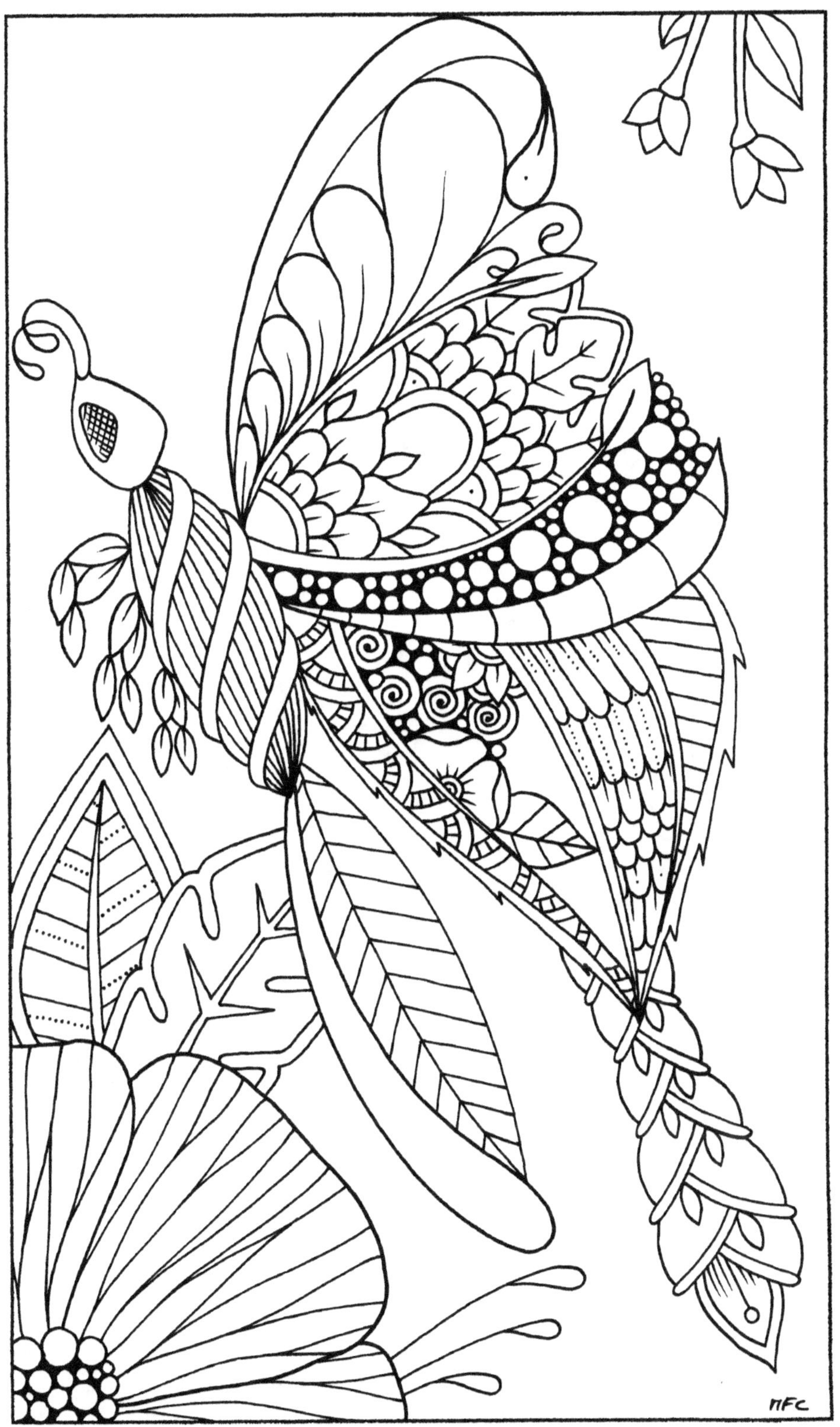

Maud FERAL CHAUVEAU - (MFC)

Enchanted Menagerie

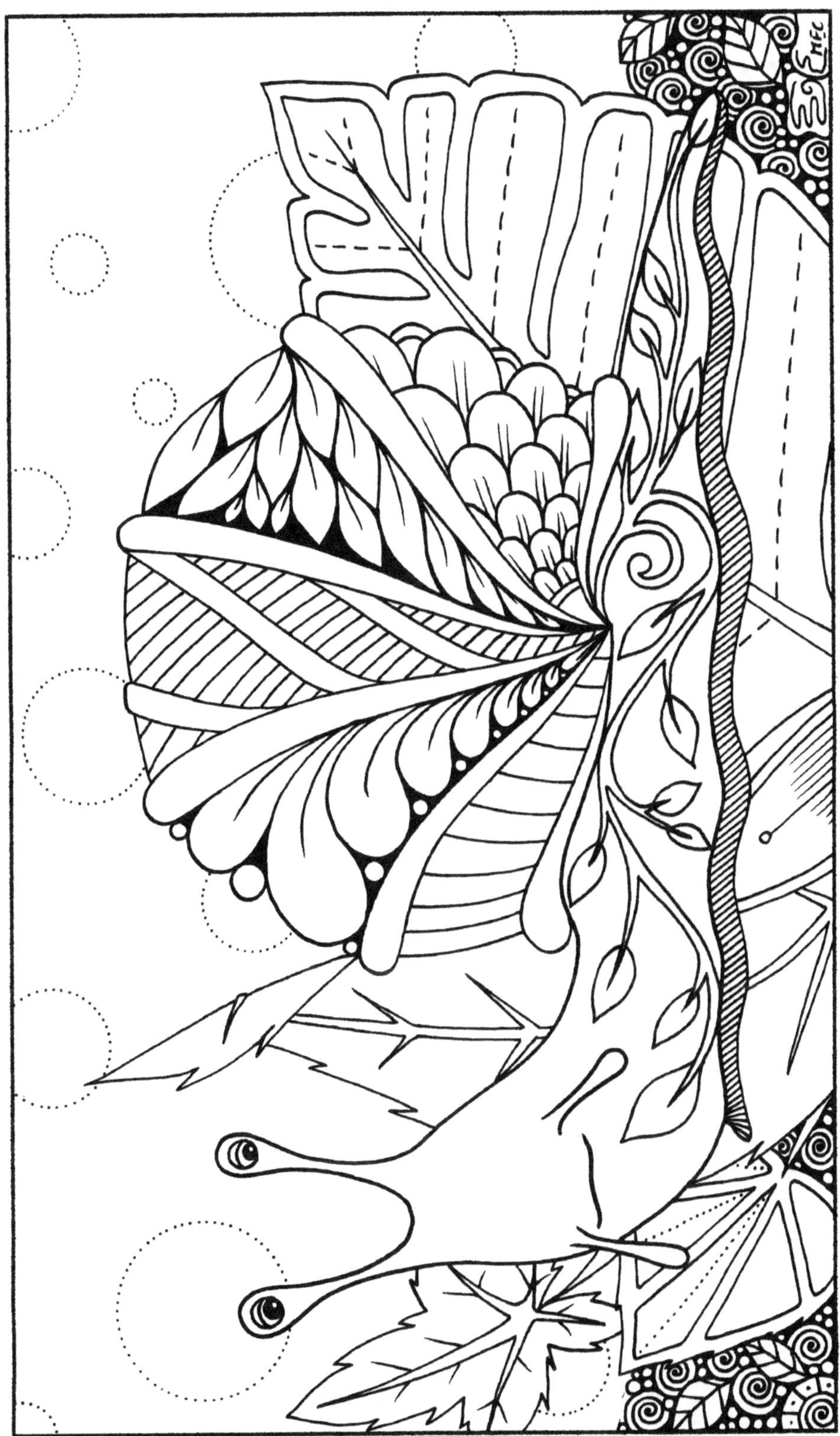

Maud FERAL CHAUVEAU - (MFC)

Enchanted Menagerie

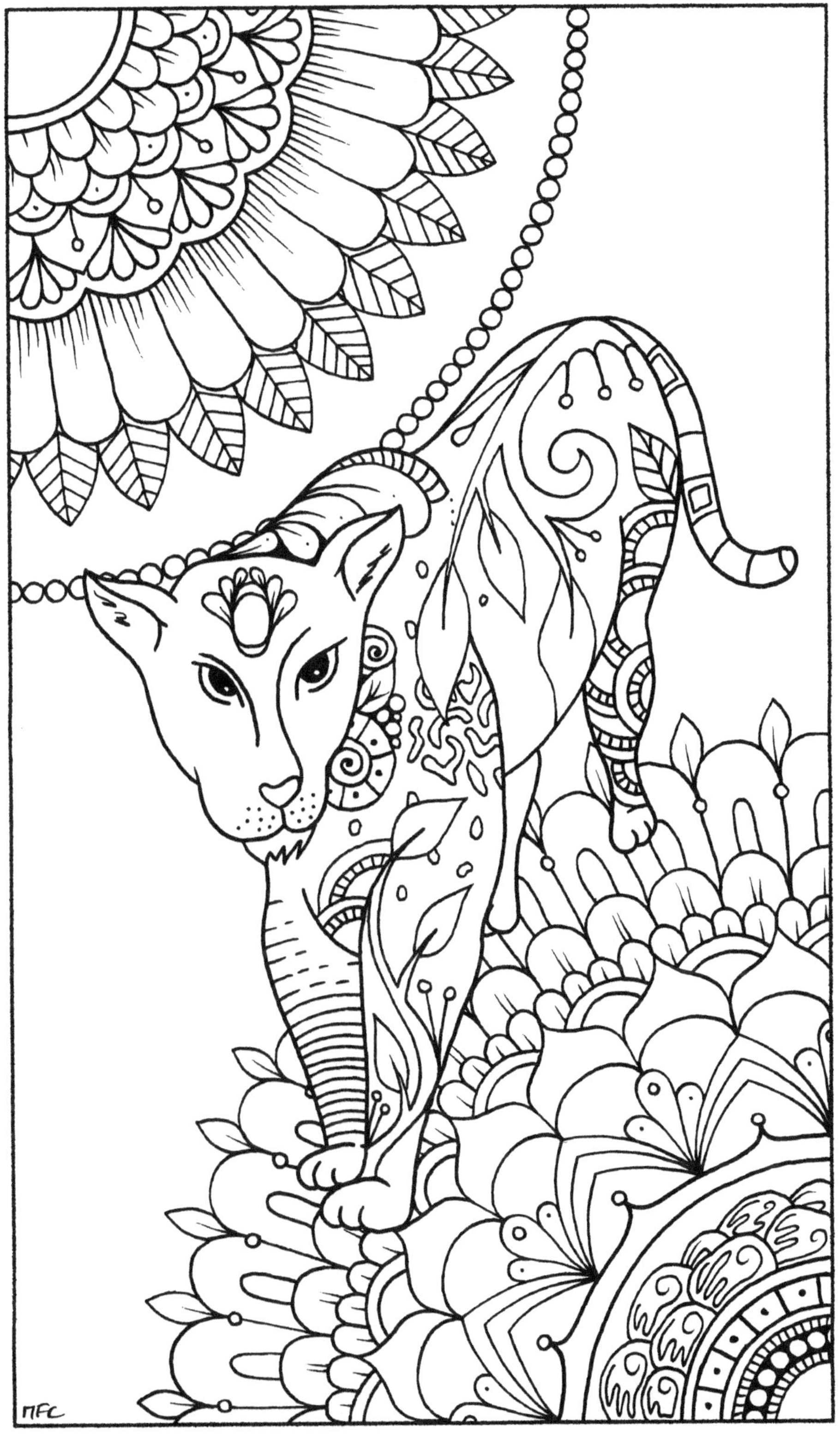
MFC

# Maud FERAL CHAUVEAU - (MFC)

## Enchanted Menagerie

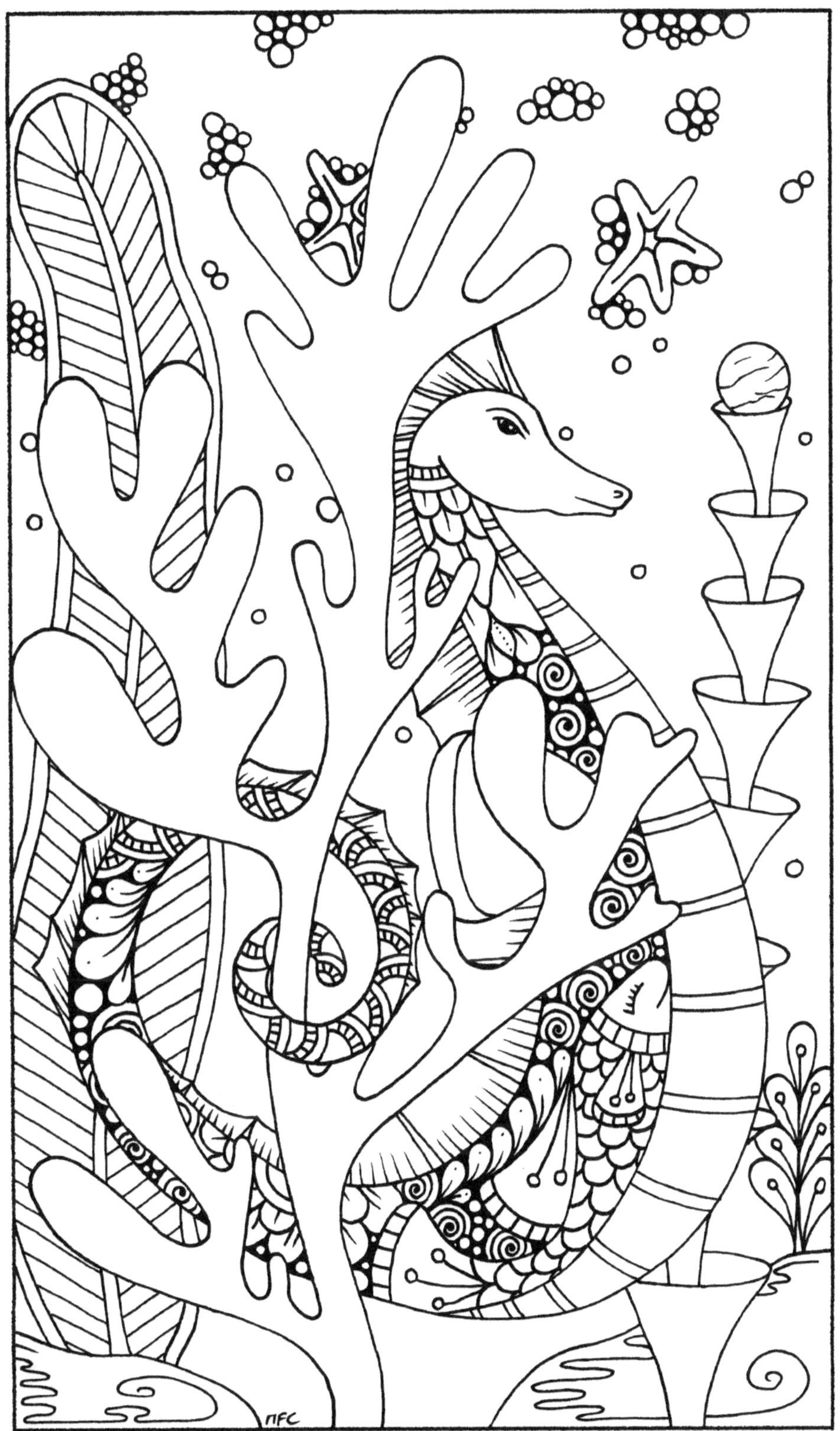

# Maud FERAL CHAUVEAU - (MFC)

## Enchanted Menagerie

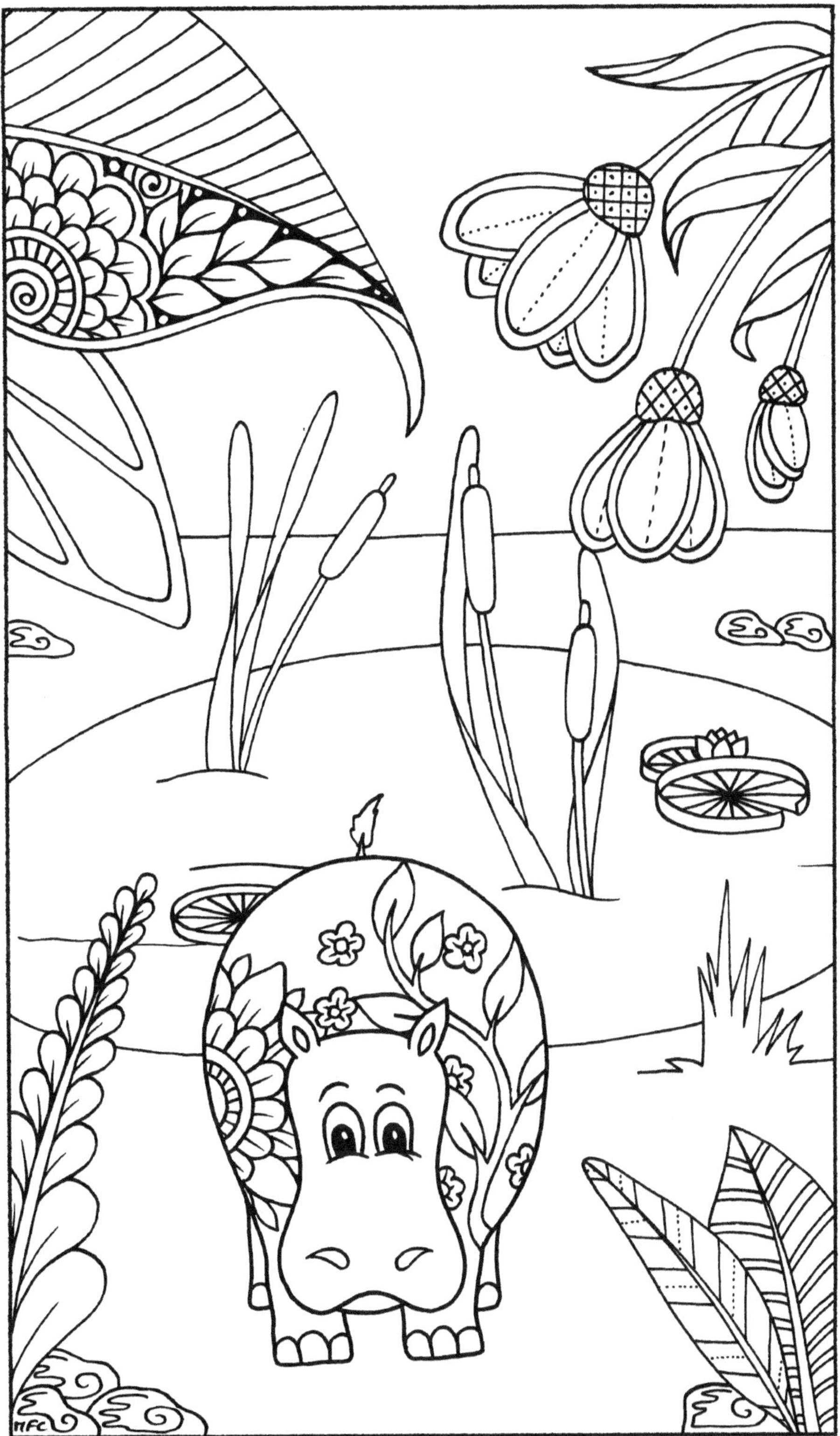

# Maud FERAL CHAUVEAU - (MFC)

## Enchanted Menagerie

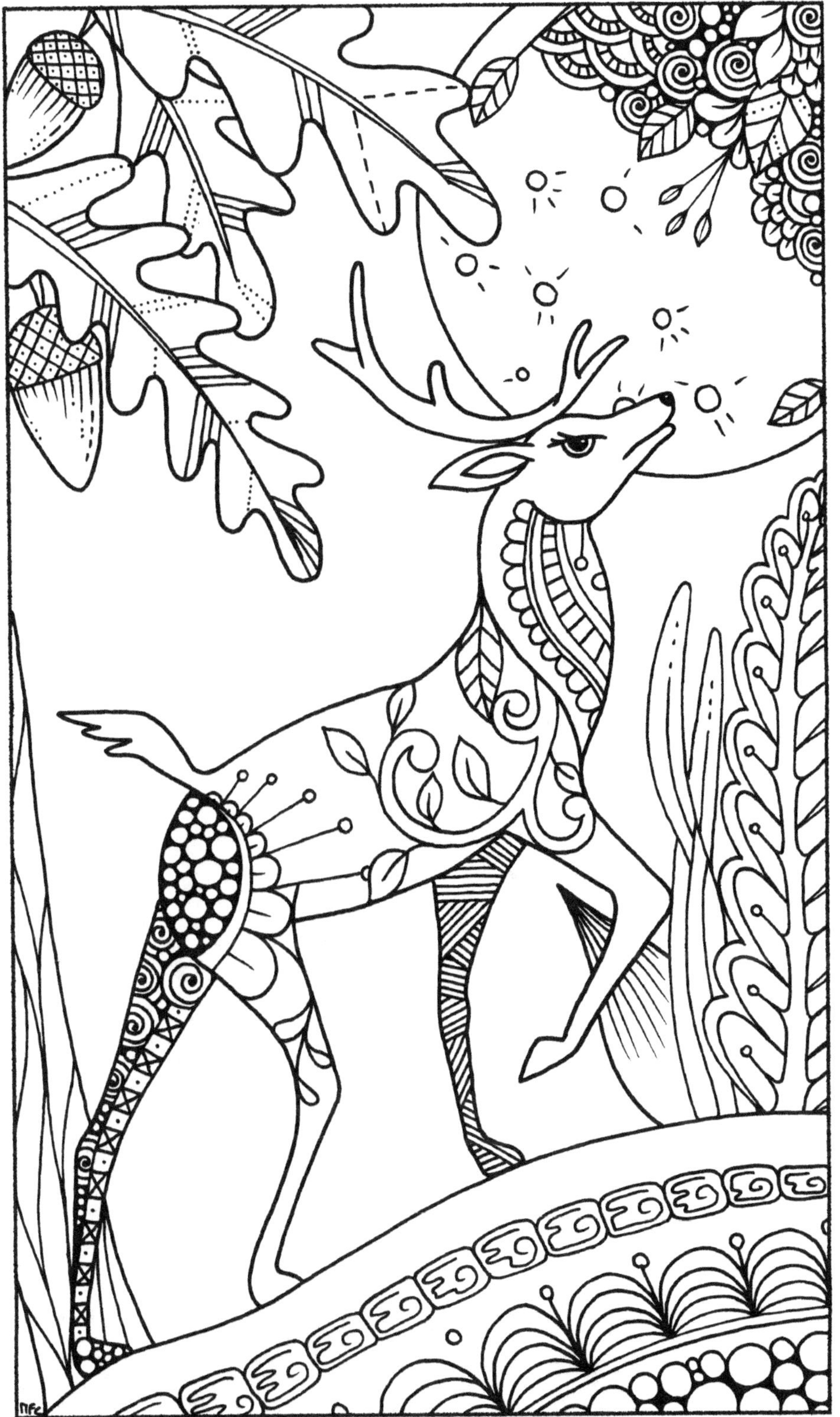

# Maud FERAL CHAUVEAU - (MFC)

## Enchanted Menagerie

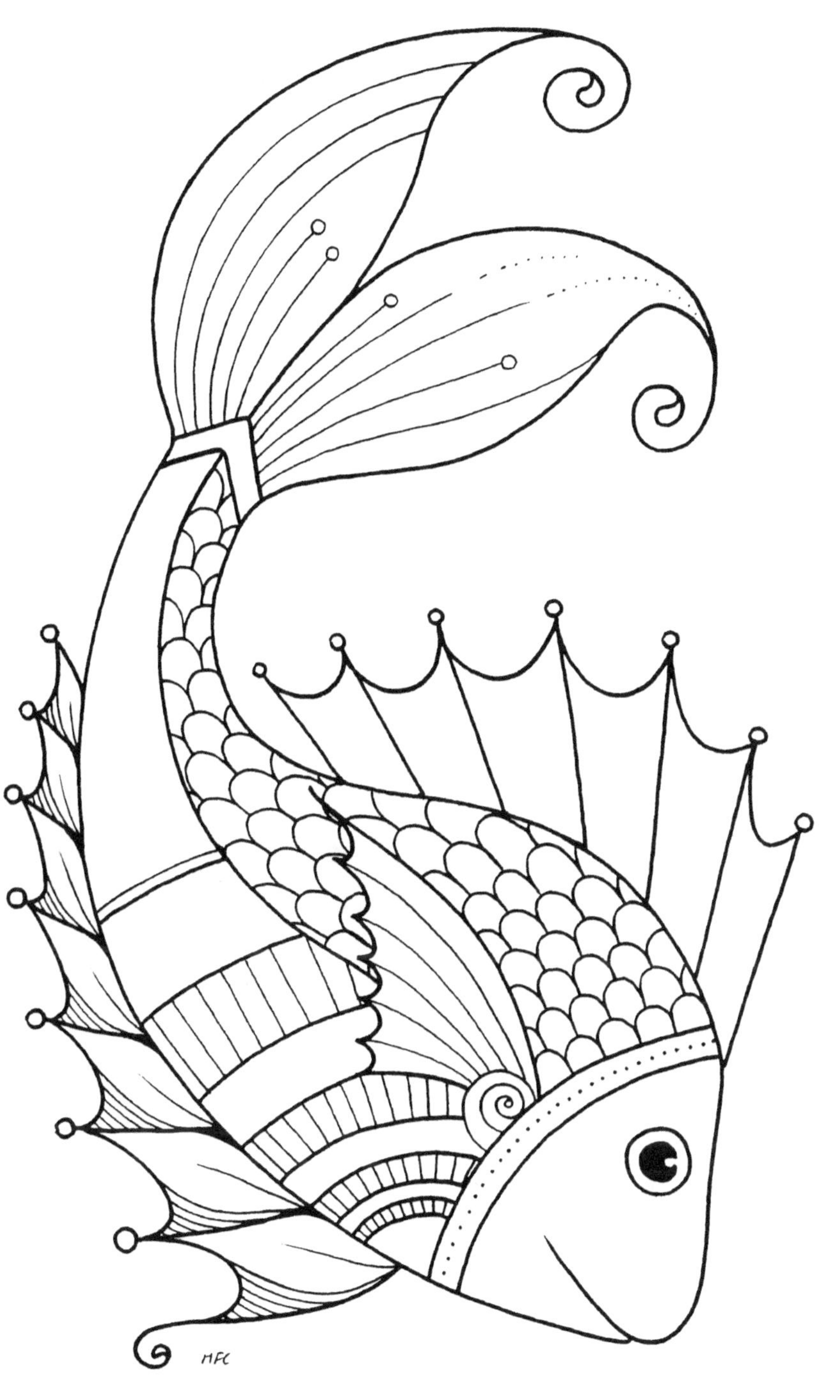

# Maud FERAL CHAUVEAU - (MFC)

## Enchanted Menagerie

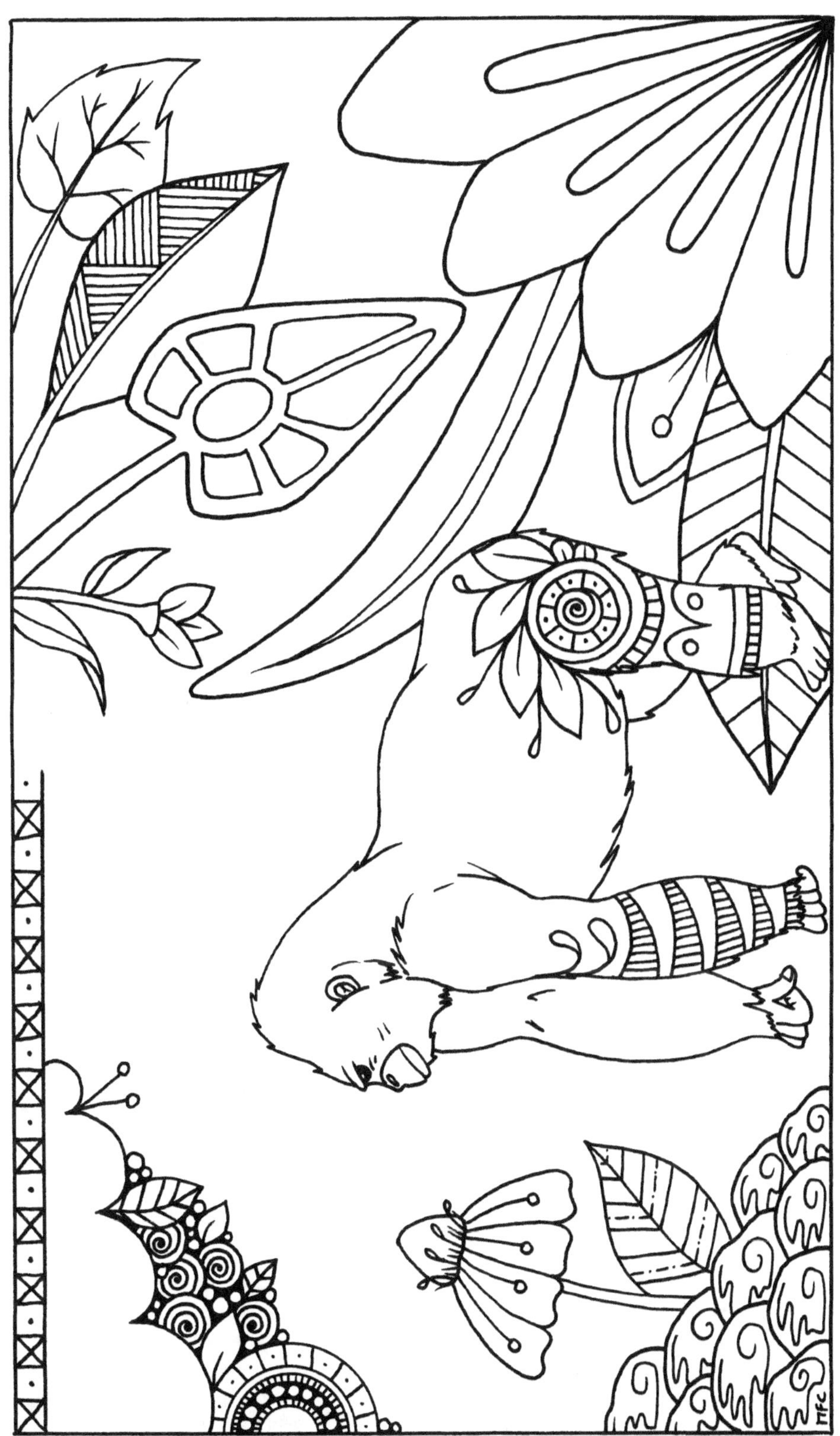

# Maud FERAL CHAUVEAU - (MFC)

## Enchanted Menagerie

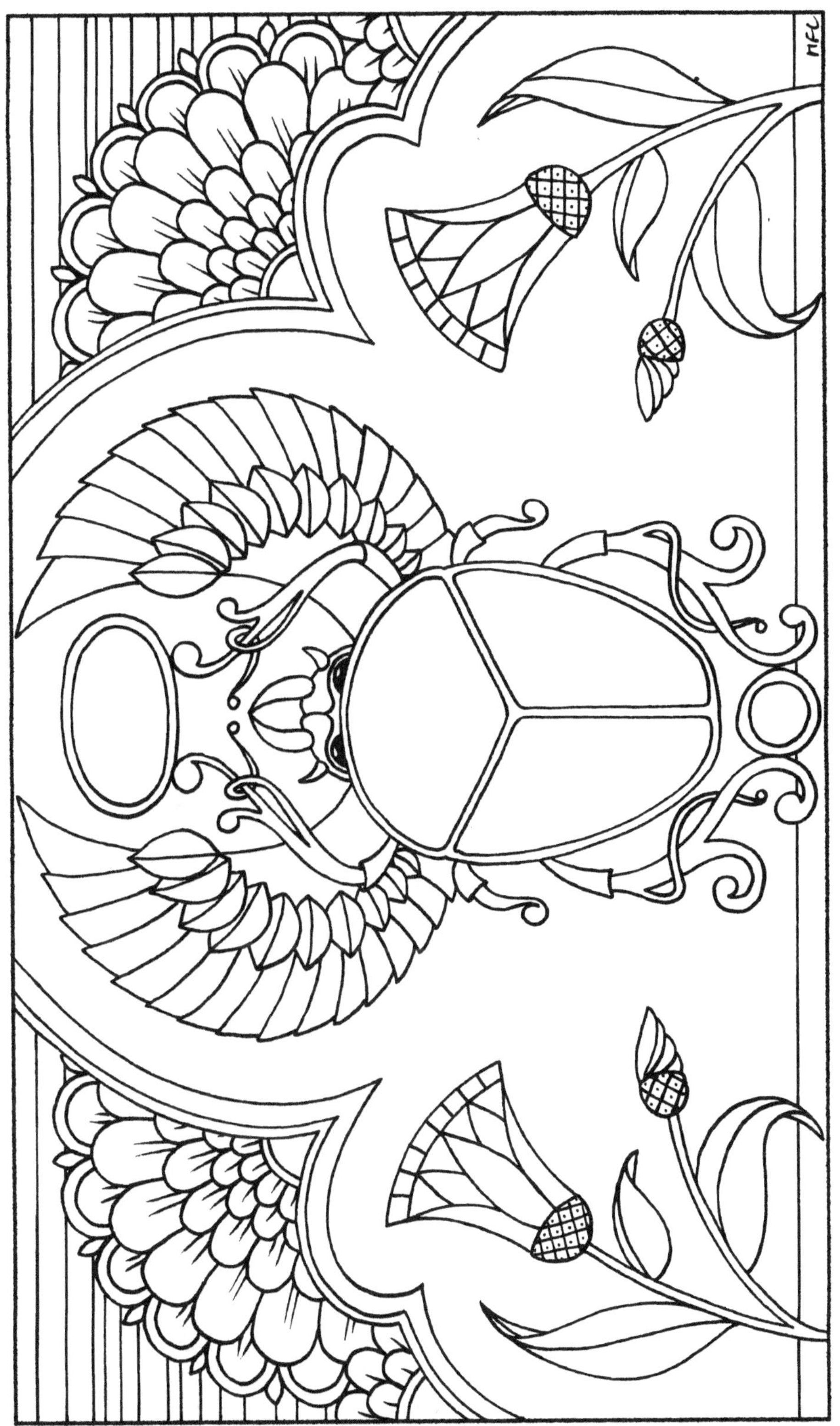

Maud FERAL CHAUVEAU - (MFC)

Enchanted Menagerie

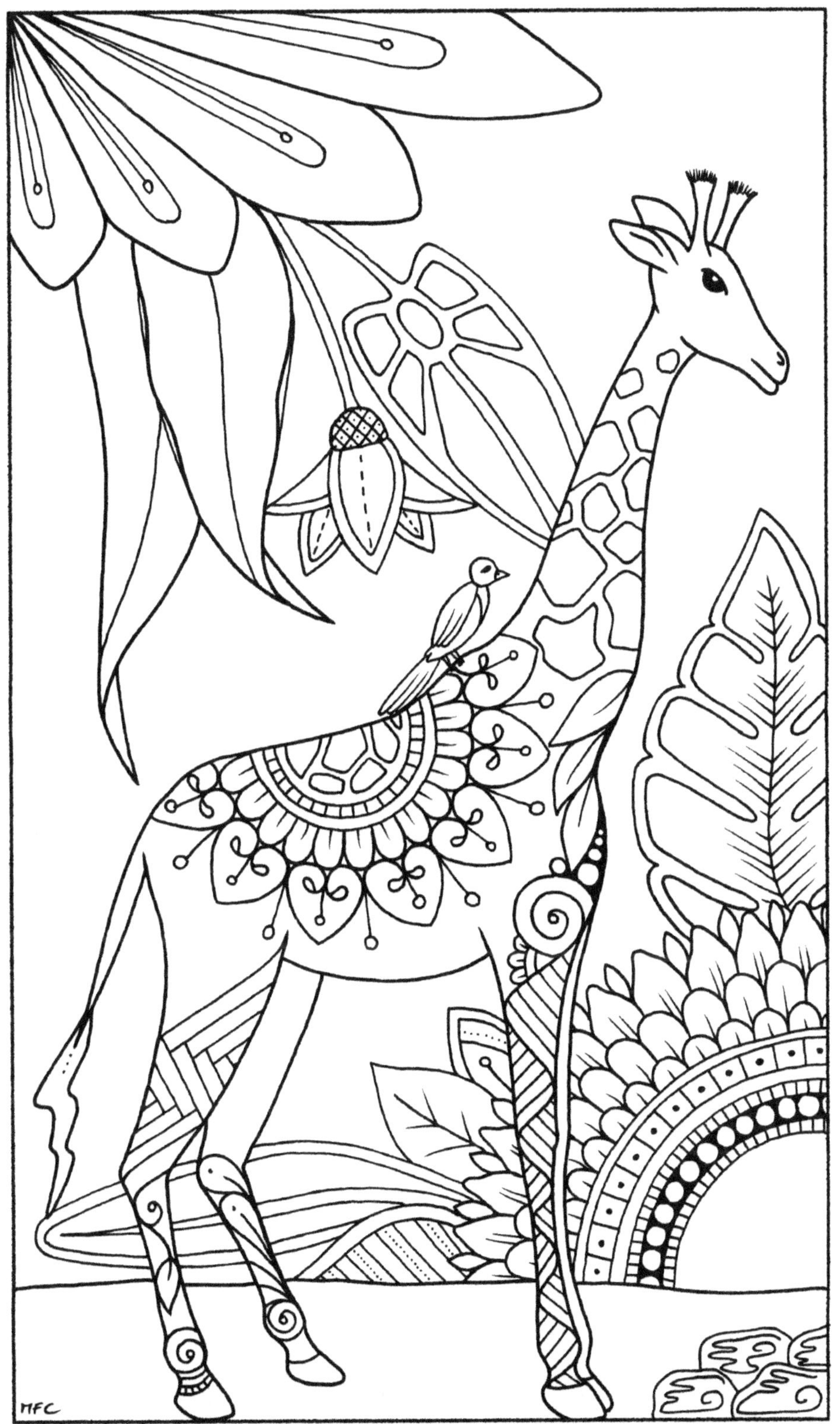

Maud FERAL CHAUVEAU - (MFC)

Enchanted Menagerie

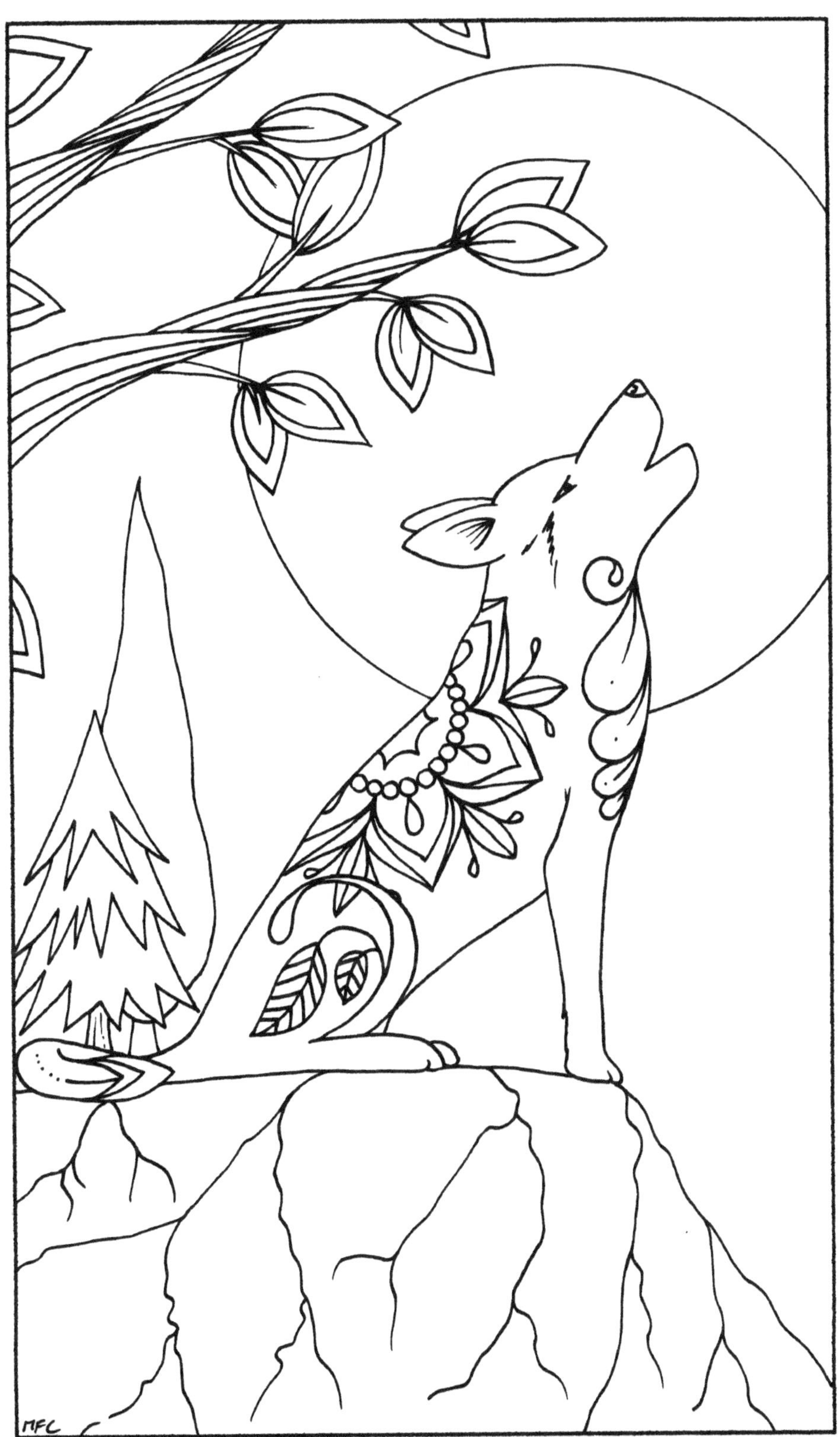

Maud FERAL CHAUVEAU - (MFC)

Enchanted Menagerie

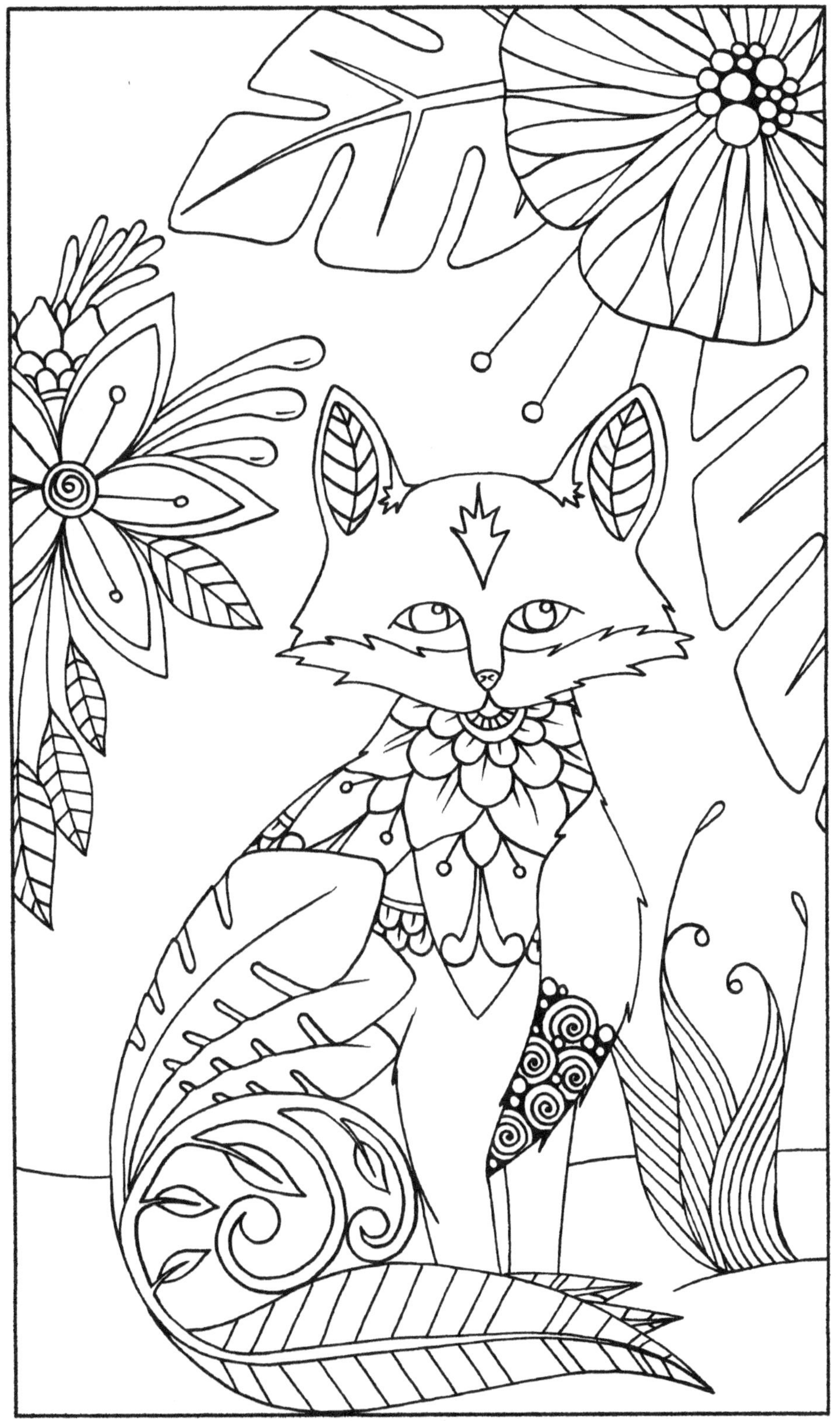

Maud FERAL CHAUVEAU - (MFC)

Enchanted Menagerie

Maud FERAL CHAUVEAU - (MFC)

Enchanted Menagerie

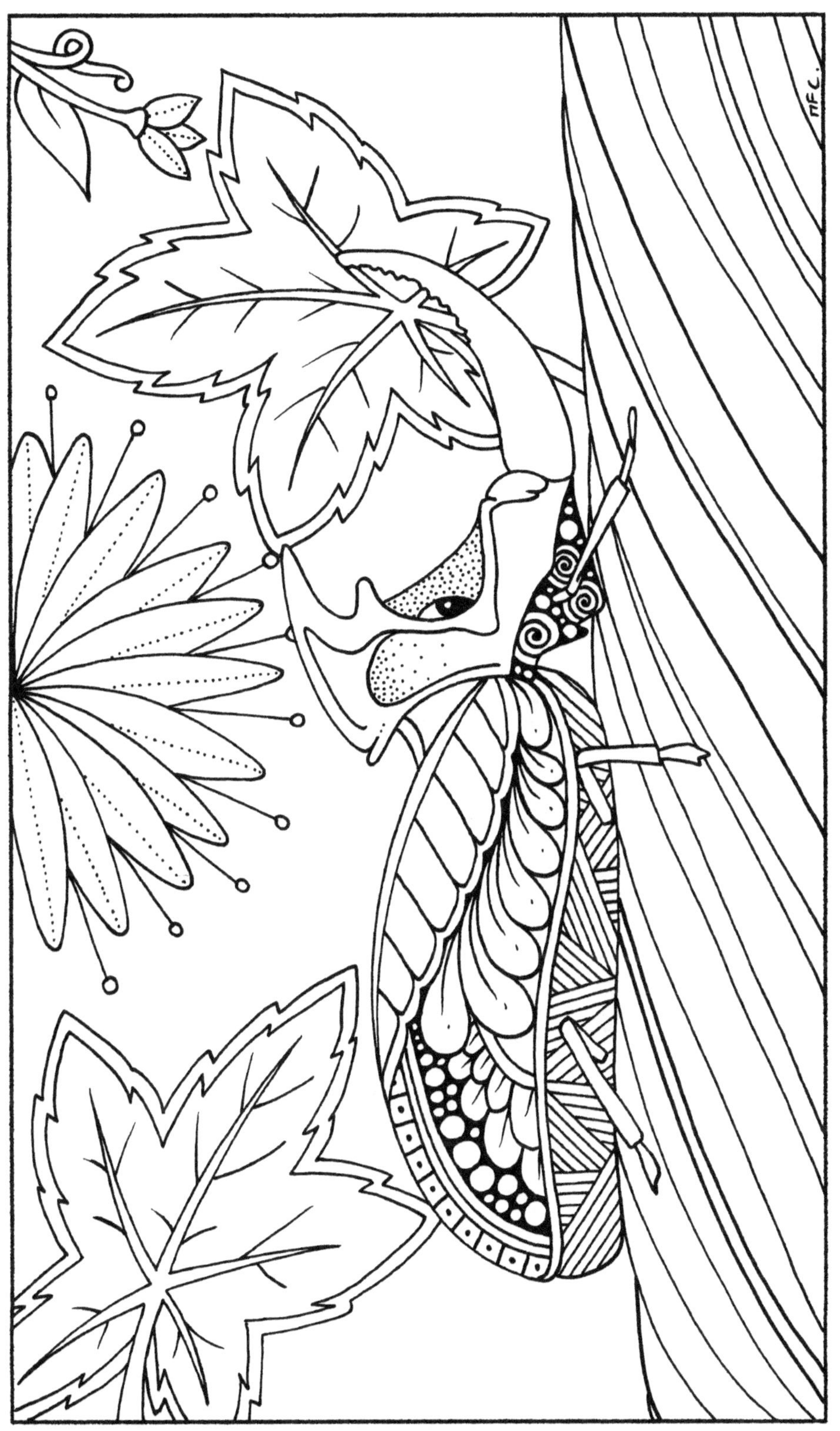

# Maud FERAL CHAUVEAU - (MFC)

## Enchanted Menagerie

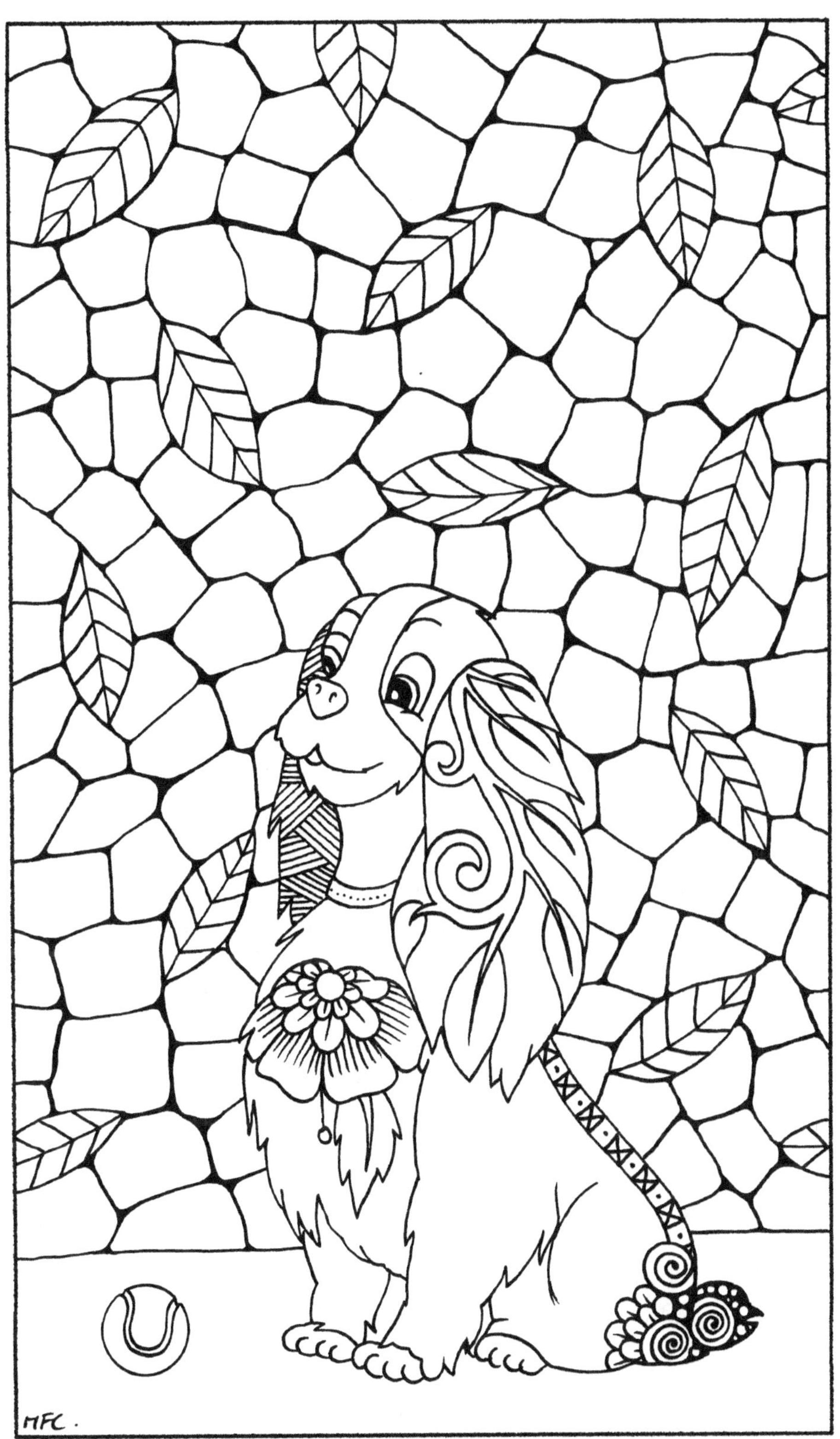

MFC.

# Maud FERAL CHAUVEAU - (MFC)

## Enchanted Menagerie

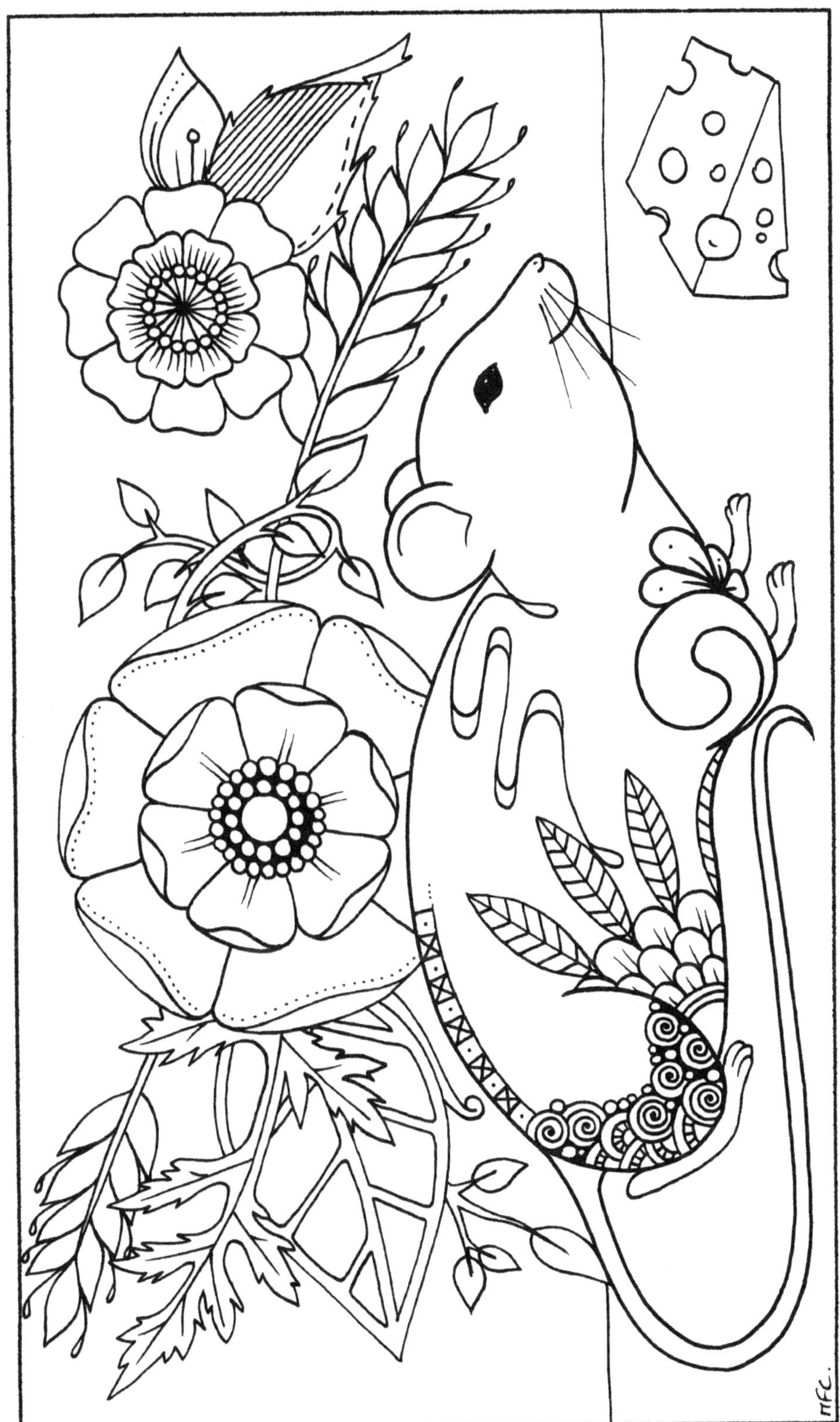

Maud FERAL CHAUVEAU - (MFC)

Enchanted Menagerie

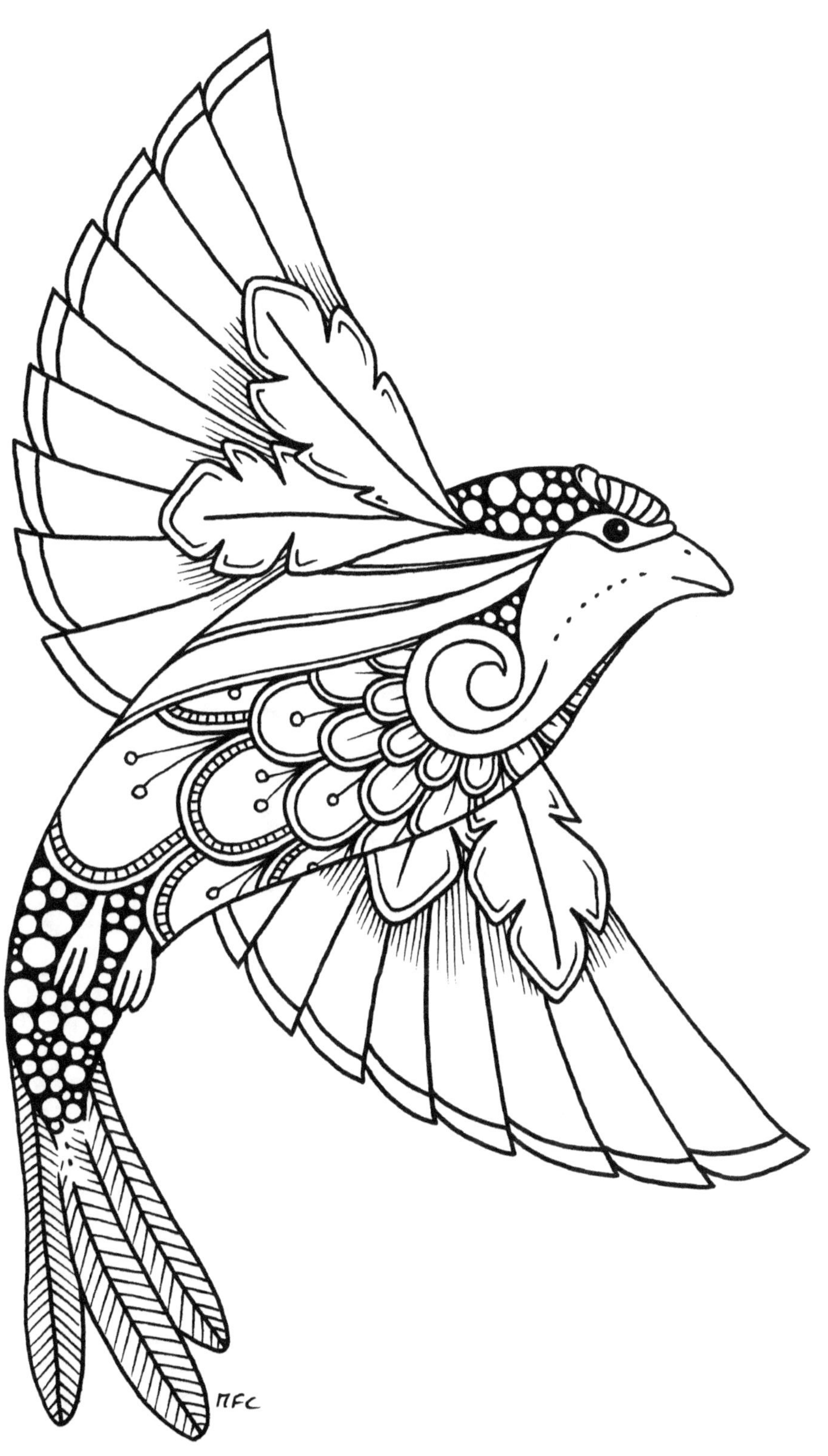

Maud FERAL CHAUVEAU - (MFC)

Enchanted Menagerie

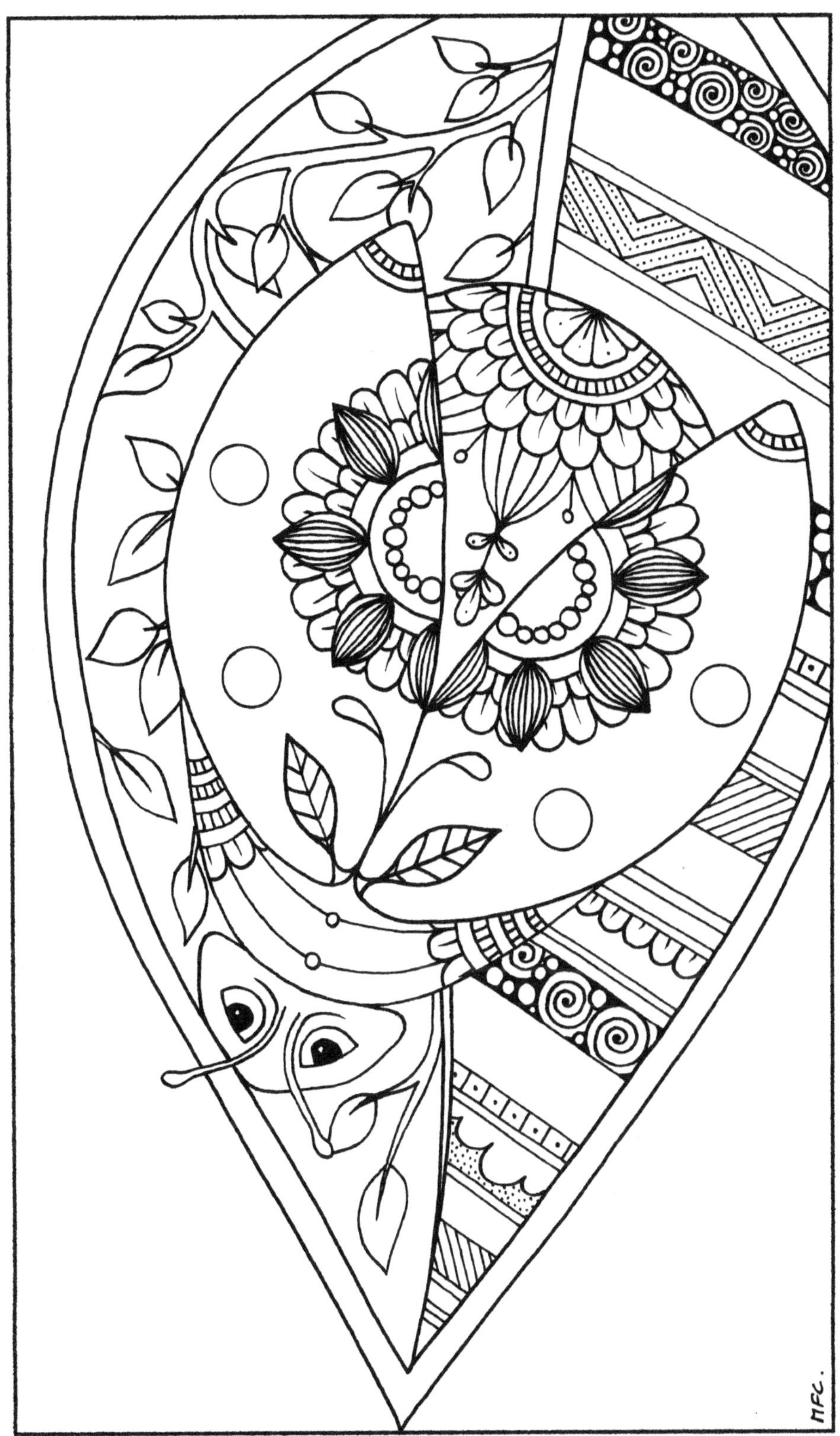

Maud FERAL CHAUVEAU - (MFC)

Enchanted Menagerie

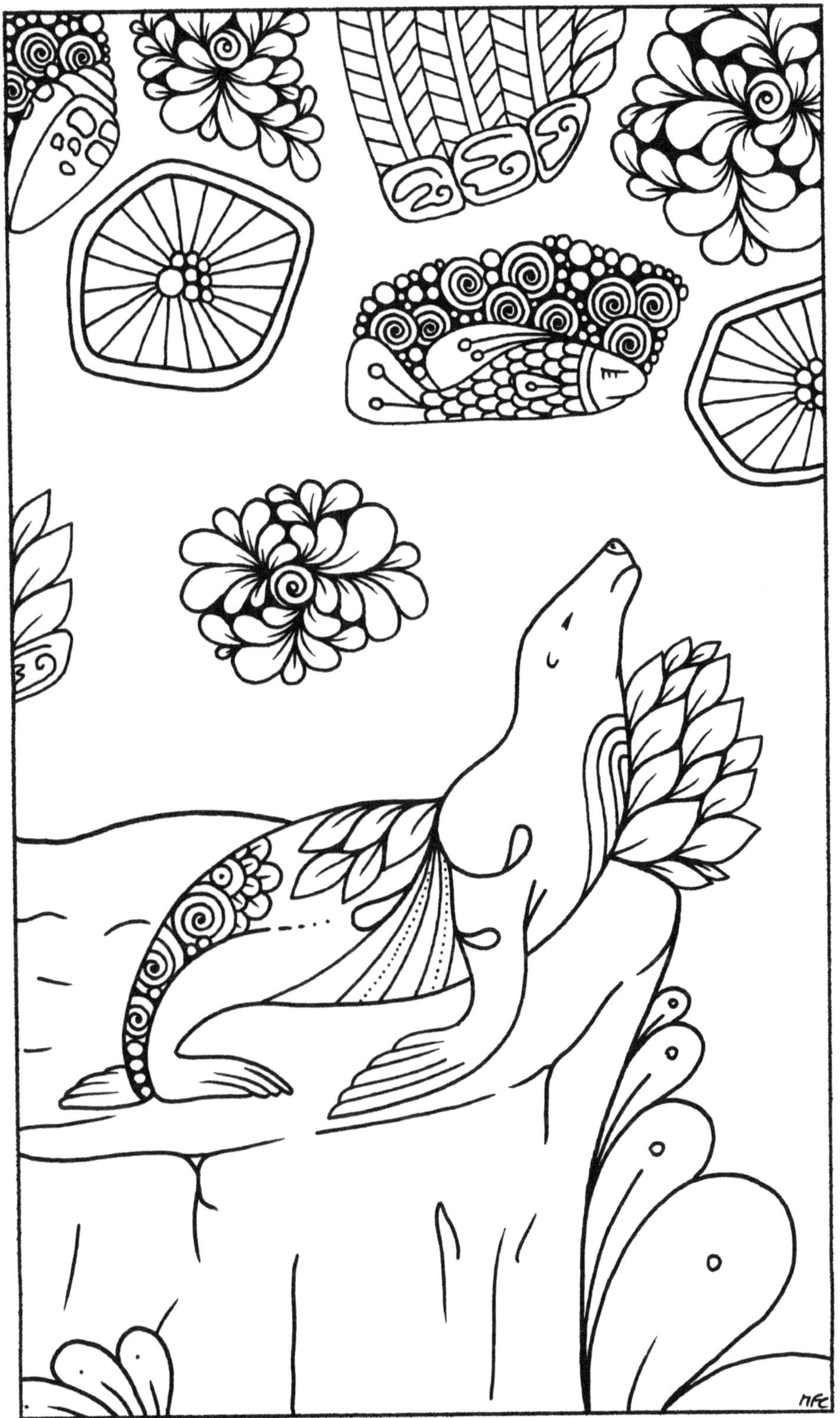

Maud FERAL CHAUVEAU - (MFC)

Enchanted Menagerie

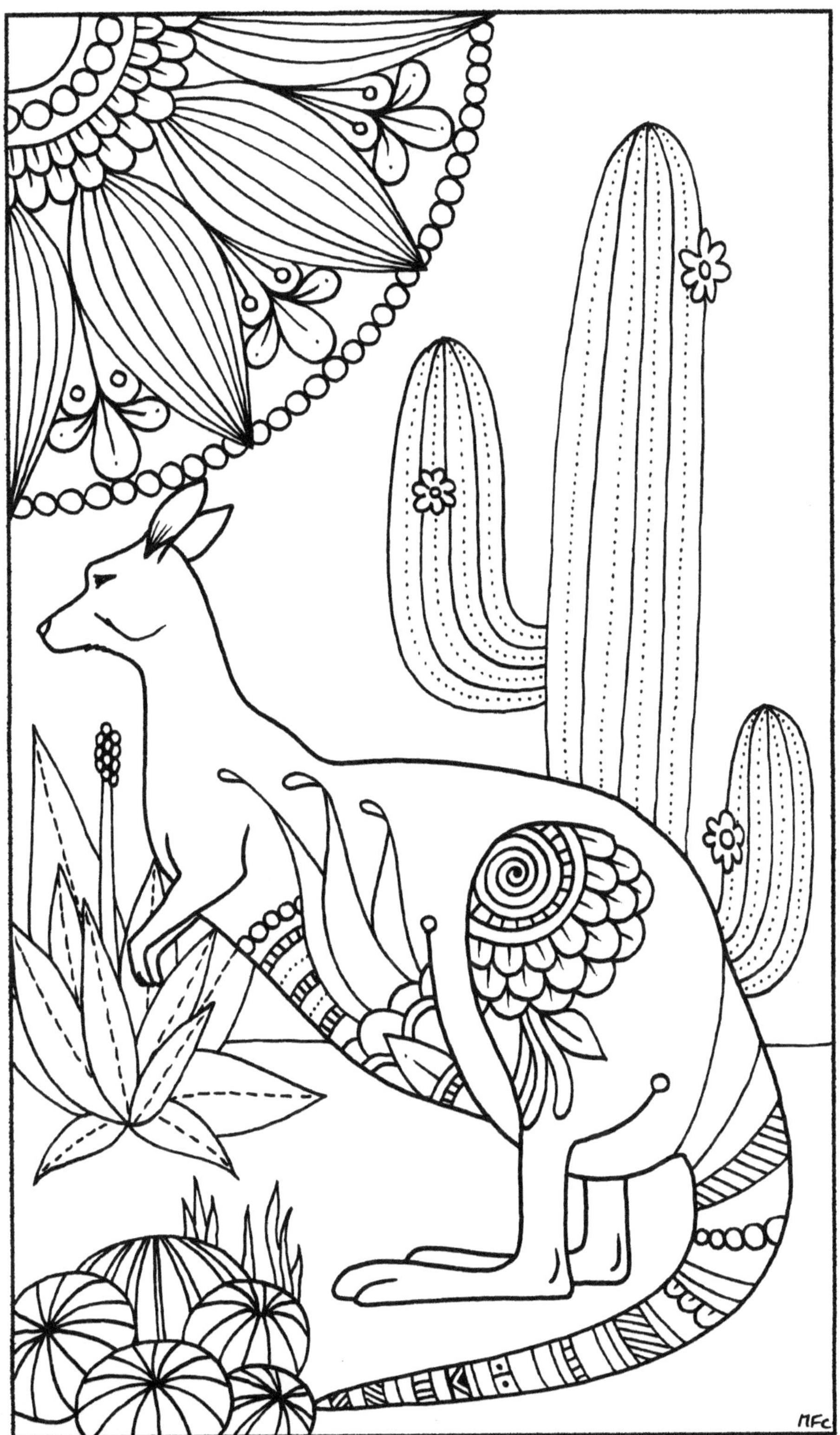

Maud FERAL CHAUVEAU - (MFC)

Enchanted Menagerie

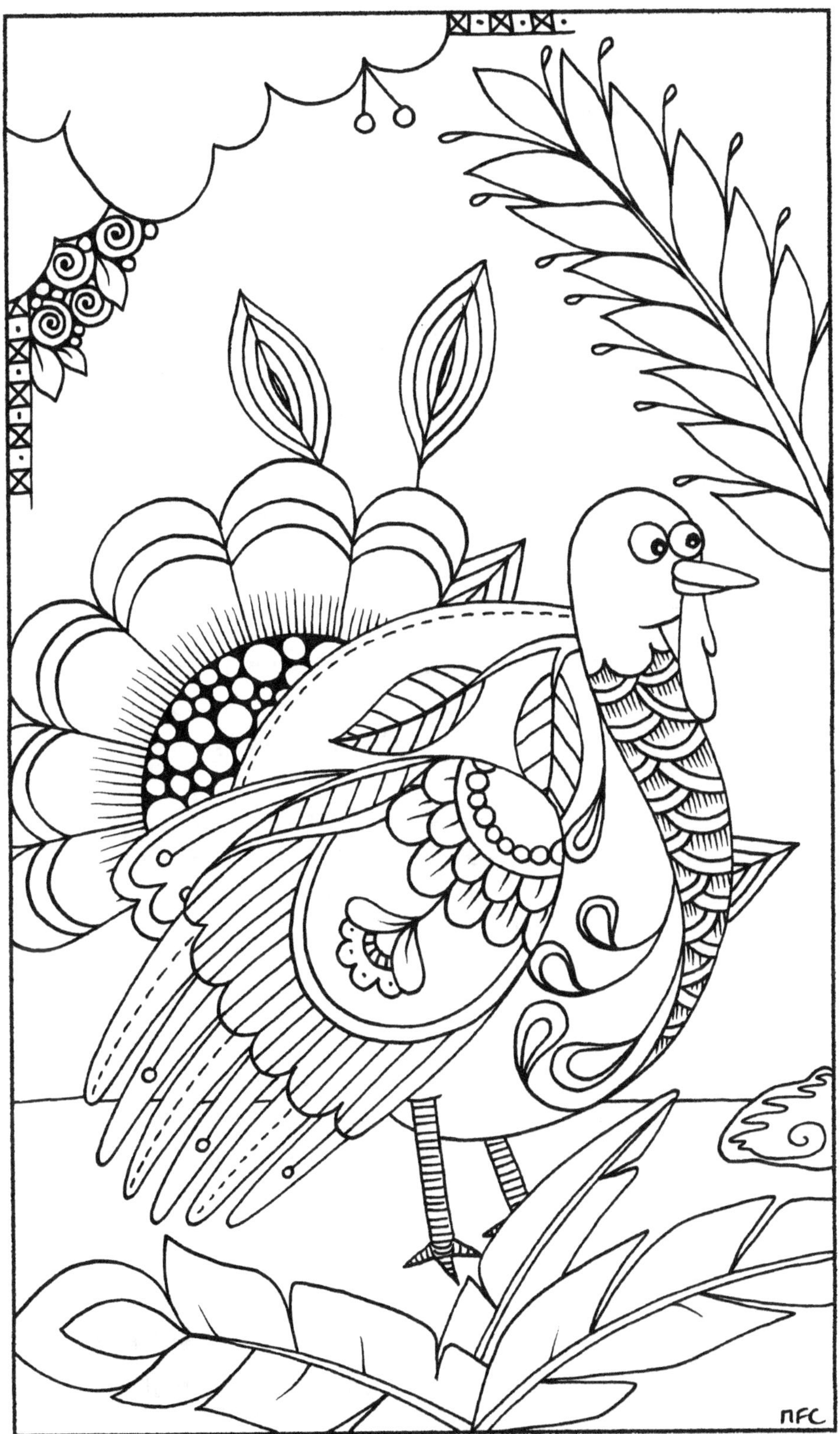

I dedicate this book to my son .
Thank you again to inspired me.

I will be really happy to see your colors and to
share with you,
also join me on my Facebook page.
See you soon

https://www.facebook.com/Maud-Feral-Chauveau-MFC-illustrations

Other books published by MFC Creations
- *The feet in the water*
- *A pencil on the heart*
- *Color your Kimmidoll*
- *Back to the sea*
- *MFC Doodles Book*

9791091517195